ALEK

Sudanese Refugee to
International Supermodel

Alek Wek

virago

VIRAGO

First published in 2007 by Virago Press

Copyright © 2007 Athian, Inc

The moral right of the author has been asserted.

A CIP catalogue record for this book
is available from the British Library.

ISBN 978-1-84408-442-5

Typeset in Bembo by M Rules
Printed and bound in Great Britain by
Clays Ltd, St Ives plc

Virago Press
An imprint of
Little, Brown Book Group
100 Victoria Embankment
London EC4Y 0DY

An Hachette Livre UK Company

www.virago.co.uk

For my father, Athian Wek, and my mother Akuol, who filled me with love. Also for my wonderful brothers and sisters: Athian, Ajok, Wek, Mayen, Adaw, Akuol, Athieng and Deng.

ACKNOWLEDGEMENTS

So many people have helped me in my journey from Sudan and back again. I give special thanks to my older sister Ajok, for giving me the opportunity to flee the civil war and emigrate to London. None of this would have been possible without her.

Mora Rowe, my first agent in New York, helped educate me as a model and as a person. She inspired me and stuck by me with good humour and strength. Thank you Mora.

Maja Edmonston, my current agent, took me under her wing at a pivotal moment. Without her I wouldn't have this book.

Chuck Bennett, Senior Corporate Vice-President of IMG Models, has always been there for me. Thanks you so much.

Many great creative people have worked with me over the years. Special thanks go to Steven Meisel, Gilles Bensimon, Herb Ritts, Nick Knight, Peter Lindbergh, Inez van Lamsweerde and Vinoodh Matadin, Arthur Elgort, Annie Leibovitz, Michael Thompson, Mark Abrahams, David LaChapelle, Richard Burbridge, Paola Roversi, John Galliano and Karl Lagerfeld.

There are so many great stylists, make-up artists and hair stylists who have helped me immeasurable throughout the years. Thanks to all of you.

Thanks also to Pirelli, Motorola Red, Barneys, Gap, Bloomingdale's, Macy's, Sephora, Saks Fifth Avenue and Ann Taylor.

My gratitude goes out to Oprah Winfrey, for her genuine words of support when we first met. Your good spirit stays with me.

Anna Wintour and her team at *Vogue* have offered me so much support throughout my career. I'm grateful for all you have done for me.

Frank Sozzani and everyone at Italian *Vogue* have been behind me from day one and continue to be there for me always. Thank you for everything.

Thanks to everyone who has helped me with WEK1933. I'm particularly grateful to Swarovski for their generous backing, both of WEK1933 and the charities we work with.

The United States Committee for Refugees and Immigrants gave me a platform to raise awareness of the plight of Sudanese and other refugees. That has been a great honour.

USCRI also introduced me to the fantastic and dedicated people at Médecins Sans Frontières.

Riccardo Sala, you've inspired me in every way. I'm so grateful.

Thanks to all my friends for your great emotional support, and to my fans who have made of all this possible. I deeply appreciate all you have done. You have given me more than I could have ever imagined.

I am thankful to Lisa Queen, my literary agent, for bringing this book to light. And thanks to Stephen P. Williams for bringing this book to life.

PROLOGUE

I was packing for the flight to London when my driver called to say he was waiting outside. I hurriedly went through my 'toss bag' of beauty products and grabbed some small bottles of moisturiser. Every week cosmetics companies send me free products, and I set aside the ones that don't work for me and give them to my sisters and friends – I don't really use much make-up, except when I'm working. I put the bottles into one of the washbags from WEK1933, the line of bags that I design. It always feels funny, yet good, to carry a bag with my father's name and year of birth engraved on the brass zipper tags – like being home again, though it's hard to say where, exactly, home would be for me. I threw the kit bag, along with a pair of jeans – also a gift, from when I did a jeans story for American *Vogue* – a couple of T-shirts and a cashmere sweater into one of my larger bags and headed for the door. On the way out I said so long to my assistant, who would be handling the business while I was away. My driver held the

1

door for me and then we headed out into the New York traffic.

I drank a cup of tea in the business class lounge before my flight. When I boarded I gulped some water and went straight to sleep. The thing about being a model is that people expect you to look fresh and bright after a transatlantic flight – no tiredness allowed.

London was my fourth home, after my home town Wau, in the southern Sudan, and a little rural village where I hid out from the fighting, and Khartoum, which was my first real home as a child refugee. So I have a soft spot for the city. I took a cab straight from Heathrow to my agent's office in Chelsea, arriving at about half-past nine in the morning. My agent and I talked for an hour about some bookings, payments and problems, and then a car rushed me to a shoot. Into wardrobe. Then hair. Then make-up, and onto the set for a full eight hours of loud music, stressed-out stylists and outlandish poses.

I had a good chat with the cockney driver as my taxi crawled across London. It's funny, but in America my British accent fades a bit and a lot of Americanisms creep in – Brooklyn hip-hop talk and the like – but as soon as I get through customs in Britain my English accent, with its full-on East London edge, returns. I love it. After all, I learned to speak English in England, on the streets of Hackney.

Back at my hotel after the shoot, I ordered a pot of tea and sank down into my bed. I felt lonely and tired – peculiar symptoms of jet lag for me – and thought of just going straight to bed, but I knew there was something better. I dressed and took a taxi over to my mother's house. Gliding through the

London streets I passed the hairdresser where I worked as a teenager. The Arab customers there used to whisper nasty remarks to each other about how skinny, dark and stupid I was, not realising that I too spoke Arabic, which was the language used at the schools I went to in the Sudan. I pretended not to understand their remarks. I needed the job.

Mum greeted me with a big smile, as always, and sat me down for supper. Two of my brothers and one sister were there and we chatted away in Dinka, the language of our people. My other five siblings were elsewhere in London, in Canada and in Australia. These days it is rare for all nine of us brothers and sisters to be together at one time but I instantly felt warm and glad I'd come. My mother served me a bowl of dried okra stew and *kissra*, a type of bread we eat, and that tasted better than any four-star meal I've ever had.

My early morning flight to Germany was cancelled and I was late for the fittings for a runway show that afternoon. The show went off well, and afterwards I rushed to my hotel to shower and get dressed for a party that evening. By ten o'clock I was exhausted and passed out on my bed.

In the morning I flew to Milan. The city was buzzing with models, make-up artists, stylists, journalists and hangers-on, all in town for fashion week – such a great vibe. I had eight shows lined up over the next few days. Backstage, journalists kept sticking microphones in my face, asking for comments on what it was like to be black, to be African, to be a black African. I started to feel like an exhibit in their zoo. In the hotel I turned on the TV. It was tuned to the Fashion Channel. There was Alek Wek, in an interview from some previous fashion week. 'It's like, wow, you know,' she said. I fell asleep, but it wasn't restful.

I awoke in the middle of the night to the sound of gunfire. I jumped out of bed and grabbed my clothes. The militias were outside. I was terrified.

Then I noticed the glow of light coming under the hotel room door. I realised where I was: a luxury hotel room in Milan. I heard the gunfire again: it was a truck collecting rubbish in the piazza below my window. I was not in the Sudan. There was no threat.

A few days later I flew back to New York. In the hall of my house I came face to face with an oil painting of a pair of sandals on a grey background. The sandals were like leather flip-flops. I'd painted them a few months before, while thinking of Wau. The sandals were the same shape as the rubber ones I used to wear as a child, the flimsy ones I wore when I was running through sharp grass, afraid that armed men were going to catch me and kill me. These leather sandals represented security and strength, when for so long there had been fearfulness and flight. I'd always wanted leather sandals as a child. And now, in this painting, I had them.

CHAPTER 1

After I was born, the seventh of nine children, my mother and I returned from hospital to her simple string bed, in a cement-block house in a little town called Wau. My parents named me Alek, after one of my beloved great aunts. Alek means 'black spotted cow', one of the most common and well-loved types of cow in the Sudan. It's also a symbol of good luck for my people, the Dinka. I got my long body from my father – I'm five feet eleven inches tall – and my mother gave me my smile. My inky skin came from both of them.

When a child is born to the Dinka the family has a party. When I was born, family and friends came from all over, thanks to the bush telegraph. There were very few telephones where I grew up, so my father mentioned my birth to some-one at the market. And that woman told a man who was delivering rice to a place up the road. He told someone there, who was taking a herd of cattle south towards the villages. And pretty soon the news of my birth had spread far and wide. Some of my relatives travelled for hours in the backs of trucks, or walked across miles of barren landscape to reach our home.

The women got together and made oils and perfumes from herbs and bark, which they soaked for days and mixed in special ways that only the elders know. As my mother tells it, the house was filled with women in their traditional robes and everything smelled wonderful. For two days these women cared for my mother and me. They fed her a special porridge and chicken soup, and wiped her brow with damp cloths. She didn't have to do anything but lie back, take special baths and luxuriate in sensual smells. Then the men brought a black goat to sacrifice, according to our tradition. Everyone ate good millet cakes and other sweets, which were such a rare treat in my family. As custom dictated, my mother stayed in the house for forty full days and nights after she gave birth to me.

It was a rare moment of peace in my country, and I was blessed with a very special welcome into the world. A Dinka welcome.

My people have lived in the southern Sudan for thousands of years. We're related to two gracile East African groups, called the Nuer and the Masai, that make up the Nilotic people, who are known for their dark skin and tall, lean bodies. There are about twenty Dinka tribes altogether, and each is divided into many smaller groups, with villages spread over a huge area. My family is from the region called Bahr el Ghazal, in the south-western part of the country. Bahr el Ghazal is also the name of a river that meanders through the swamps and ironstone plateaux until it joins the White Nile at a lake called, simply, No. The White Nile goes on to meet the Blue Nile at

Khartoum, and proceeds from there to Egypt in the river we know as the Nile.

Based on the stories my parents and grandparents told, it seems that the Sudan has always been a violent land. In the eighteenth and nineteenth centuries slave traders came through this territory, nabbing Dinkas and others and taking them north to be sold in the Arab countries. It is said that children from the south have even been enslaved and sold in the twenty-first century.

The main thing to understand about my country is that it has always been split between the Islamic Arab north and the Animist and Christian south. They don't ever seem to mix that well and the north has always tried to dominate the south. The British, who ruled the Sudan from the late nineteenth century until the 1950s, governed the north and south separately, but in the 1940s, just before independence, the British gave in to pressure from the Islamic leaders in the north to unite the country. The northern government then proceeded to impose Islamic culture on the southern people, most of whom weren't Muslim or Arabic. Of course, there's money involved too. The Sudan's vast oil fields are in the south, along with a lot of fertile land and water.

The south has never wanted to be dominated by the Muslims in the north; in 1956 a brutal civil war broke out and lasted until 1972. Then, in that year, both sides signed the Addis Ababa Accord, which guaranteed autonomy for the southern Sudan. I was born five years later.

Since we've always been semi-nomadic, totally dependent on the weather and whipped by the forces of political change around us, the Dinka are used to living through cycles of wars and uprisings followed by peace and prosperity, hunger and then bounty. In the wet season rural Dinka out in the villages live in conical, thatch-roofed huts, growing millet and other crops. In the dry season they take their cattle to riverside camps. Us Dinka are born expecting change.

The Dinka have never had a central government or anything like that, except those imposed on use by the leaders of the Sudan. Instead, we are divided into clans, which are based on families, and Dinka are very aware of which clan they belong to. Some of the more important clans will have leaders who influence the whole tribe. But in general, the clans are split into smaller groups and each of these will have control of just enough land to provide water and pasture for their beloved cattle.

These animals are so essential to the Dinka that even though my parents raised us in a small, relatively cosmopolitan town, far from their home villages, my mother still kept about fifteen head of long-horned cattle in our courtyard.

Like my father Athian Wek, my mother Akuol Parek grew up in a thatched hut in a village south of Wau. My mother has a different name because in our culture children always take – and keep – their father's name. By the time my parents married the civil war between the north and south was in full force and they had to flee. They roamed Africa, living for long periods of time in refugee camps and towns and cities in Kenya, the Central African Republic and elsewhere. That was just how life was for them. They had to build a life on the run, so to speak.

My mother gave birth to her first children while she was in exile. When peace eventually came to the south my parents returned to the Sudan and settled in Wau, which was then a town of about seventy thousand people, roughly three hundred miles from the Ugandan border. They chose Wau because it was quite sophisticated, compared to the villages where they had grown up. While they had a deep respect for their Dinka inheritance, their time as refugees had shown my parents more of the world than they would otherwise have seen. They realised that they wanted their children to have a good education and the freedom to marry who they wanted: most marriages in the villages were arranged. In fact, my mother defied her parents to marry my father, who wasn't deemed to come from a family that was wealthy enough. My parents saw that the Sudan, and the world at large, was in the midst of a great transition and they wanted us to be raised free from some of the more restrictive Dinka tribal customs – such as polygamy and facial scarring – so we could prosper in the modern world. They chose to settle in Wau which, while having a large Dinka population that was respectful of its tribal customs, had good schools and businesses.

Wau had originally been settled by slave traders in the nineteenth century, but had become a centre for trading cotton, tobacco, peanuts, cereals, fruit and vegetables, and also had a few small workshops. I loved walking by the blacksmith's shop, where the smiths forged metal over fires built into holes in the ground. They'd heat the metal until it was glowing red and then bang it with a hammer.

A lot of Dinka lived there, but so did a lot of Fertit, Jo-Luo, and Arab Muslims from the north. It is a diverse place, where people really get along – at least when they aren't at war with each other. Much of the town was destroyed in anti-government riots in 1965. The government rebuilt the buildings, including a strategically important airport, after the peace treaty of 1972. There was one modest hotel and a little cinema. By the time I was born, in 1977, Wau was a nice small town where women shopped for food in the market and vultures prowled the streets looking for scraps.

I grew up in what was considered a middle-class family in Wau. The middle class was fairly large in the town and was mostly made up of doctors, teachers and government workers who lived in houses made of stone and zinc. There were plenty of people poorer than us, who lived in neighbourhoods where the houses had thatched roofs and the adults worked in the fields or did other hard labour. There weren't that many people who were richer than us, aside from a handful who owned local factories or other businesses. I always felt very comfortable with what we had, although most people in Europe or America would have called us poor, since we didn't have electricity or an indoor toilet, let alone a stereo, a TV or any kitchen appliances. We had enough to eat, a solid house and simple clothes. For that we felt fortunate. Before I was born Wau had running water, but the government cut if off at some point and the system fell into disrepair. After that, everyone had to rely on well pumps. It wasn't a bad life at all. You just had to know how to make the most of what you had. We painted an old oil drum in our yard in bright colours and used it to collect the rain that fell on our roof. That rainwater tasted delicious.

My father Athian worked at the local board of education. He left the house each morning wearing a suit and tie and carrying a black leather briefcase. He was a very stylish man, about six feet five inches tall, slender and handsome. A real gentleman. He didn't talk much, but when he spoke he was always straightforward. He expected you to listen to what he had to say and I learned early on that even though he was usually easygoing he wasn't one to mess with.

I remember once he told me to go out and sweep the veranda, but I refused. Without a word he stepped into the yard, pulled a switch from a bush, and made me stand in front of him as he peeled off each leaf and twig to make a good whip. Then he lashed the backs of my legs three times and told me to never disobey him again. I don't think I ever did.

My mother Akuol was always talking, always smiling, but she was also strict. My parents were a good match. They'd known each other since they were teenagers and a deep river of trust ran between them. Dinka men can sometimes be domineering, and my father was no slouch as the man of the house, but he was different from other Dinka men. For instance, he chose not to be polygamous, even though he could easily have done so since taking multiple wives is accepted – even expected – in Dinka culture. He always consulted my mother before making big decisions. They were a real team. Except when it came to money. In that respect my mother was the dictator of the family. On payday my father would hand his money straight over to her and she would organise the rent and buy the food.

A few times a year she would take us to the market to buy clothes. Sometimes they would be new; other times we'd buy from the vendors who bought used clothes by the pound and sold them by the piece in little towns like ours. These are the same clothes that people in wealthy countries dump into collection boxes. We would often wear strange shirts advertising Manchester United football team or Jimmy's Rib Joint in Harrison, Kentucky. We didn't care: the clothes were inexpensive but well made and we couldn't read much English anyway.

My father was so tall it was difficult to find clothes to fit him. My mother would pick up some fabric swatches from a vendor in the market and they would decide whether he wanted a lightweight suit or one in a more formal fabric, checked or striped, and then they'd go to the tailor.

In the evenings my father would sit in a shaded chair on the veranda and have a cup of tea while he listened to the BBC World Service on his little battery-powered radio. Sometimes I would sit with my father and listen to the radio, but usually my mother would intervene and tell me to finish my homework. Education was very important to my parents and my father would back her up completely.

'What did you learn today?' he asked me every night at dinner. 'Did you learn how to rule the world?'

'No,' I would have to say.

'Well then, get in there and do your homework.'

And that's what I did.

We lived in a two-bedroom house with a veranda and a walled-in courtyard with a garden and space for the cows. There were four boys in the men's bedroom with my father and five girls in the women's bedroom with my mother.

The boys were: Athian, who was born in 1961, in my father's home town, Kwajok; Wek, who was born in Liberia in 1966; Mayen, who was also born in Liberia, in 1969, and Deng, who was born in Wau in 1982. He's the tallest of the bunch now, at six feet and seven inches, compared to my measly five feet eleven inches.

Besides me, the girls were: Ajok, who was born in Uganda in 1964; Adaw, who was born in Uganda in 1972; Akuol, who was born in Uganda in 1974 and given our mother's name; and Athieng, who was born in Wau in 1979.

By the time I was a young girl Ajok, Wek and Athian had grown up and left home, either to study or to live in Khartoum. When I was nine years old Ajok was living in London with her husband, a Sudanese man who was training as an architect over there. There were still plenty of us children to keep our parents busy.

Our yard consisted of hard-packed dirt, which kept snakes and other animals away. There were papaya and mango trees out there, and my mother kept a few rows of okra and tomato plants. There was no plumbing or electricity so we used an outhouse in the courtyard, with newspaper or leaves instead of toilet paper. In the kitchen there were a few stew pots and a griddle. Our rooms were furnished with stools and chairs, and we slept in beds made of woven string.

I can't say that we had much in the way of luxuries, except that we had more than a lot of people. Poverty is relative and, compared to many people, those who sometimes had trouble putting food on their tables, we were doing really well. Yet we also had neighbours who had generators for electricity, hot running water and other comforts we couldn't imagine having. The truth was, we never thought about these things. We rarely feasted but we never went hungry. We always had clothes, even if they were hand-me-downs.

I grew up in the typical Dinka way, following my mother from here to there until I started school. She had a strong entrepreneurial spirit, and was constantly trying to make money on the side. She always had something growing in the garden that she'd sell. Or she would lease land and raise crops such as peanuts to sell in the market. She even brewed liquor in a makeshift still. People loved to buy her liquor, which was pure and strong and tasted good – so they said. She never drank it and I never tried it. My father did, however. Occasionally he would meet his friends for a drink or two. My mother would always be furious with him.

'What did I tell you?' she'd shout. 'What are you drinking for?'

My dad would just kind of smile and tell her that he'd have a drink once in a while if he wanted to and if she didn't like it she should just go on about her business and let him be. He so rarely drank it wasn't really an issue, but my mother hated people being drunk on principle. To her, it was as bad as being lazy.

There was always work to be done. Every morning my mother would get up before everyone else and milk her cows. Then she'd wake us up and give us a cup of tea and a bit of bread, which is usually all we had for breakfast – we never ate more than two meals a day and often ate only one, or even none, if money was tight or if nothing was ripe in the garden. This was the accepted way to eat and nobody thought twice about it. It takes a long time to die of starvation and I learned early on not to complain if we were forced to miss a meal, or even a few of them. A bit of hunger isn't going to kill a person, even if it does sap your strength and spirit. It certainly makes you appreciate the food that you do receive. After drinking our tea we would make our beds and tidy up the rooms. Then we'd sweep the house and wash the floors before going out into the yard.

'Don't forget to pick up the manure,' my mother would say.

Now, the Dinka have a special relationship with cows and so the thought of picking up manure isn't such a bad one for us. Cow dung is really quite clean – after all, it is just grass and

14

water. And it's not just the dung. Sometimes, a village boy herding cattle will stick his head under a cow when it's urinating so that the liquid goes over his hair and body. That's because cow urine kills lice and keeps mosquitoes away. It's just a different way of looking at the world. If you think about it, isn't that boy clever to take care of his infestation that way, since medicines and insecticides are so scarce in the countryside?

It didn't really bother me to reach down and pick up the manure with my hands and throw it into a pile in the corner of the yard. It didn't even smell bad. We'd leave the manure to dry while we went to school and then in the evening we would burn it so the smoke would keep the flies and mosquitoes away. Then we'd rub the ashes onto the cows' skin to keep the ticks at bay. Sometimes would use the ash – which had been purified by being burned – as toothpaste. We didn't have plastic brushes in those days; we chewed on sticks until they went soft and then we would rub them along our teeth and gums. The sticks worked well on their own, but worked even better with the powdered dung. Years later, when I was twenty-six, I went to the dentist for the first time. He said that I had incredibly healthy teeth, so I'm definitely an advocate of sticks and dung powder for good oral health! Although I admit that when I left Africa I started using a toothbrush and toothpaste, since I no longer had cows.

My mother was full of love, and treated us well. In general, Dinka children are expected to listen to their elders and keep their mouths shut. This is especially true in the villages. My parents were usually pretty easygoing and didn't demand too much of us, but they did expect us to be respectful. My mother loved us but raised us with an iron fist – sometimes backed up by a stick she'd use if we got too far out of line. Still somehow, when I was young, I got it in my head that I could do what I liked. I was a tomboy, always climbing trees and walls and sometimes I just wouldn't listen. I liked a girl called Sarah who lived near us and sometimes I'd sneak out after dark, climbing over the back walls until I got to her house, so we could play games and sing songs in her yard. One night I came home streaked with dirt from the packed-dirt walls and my mother said, 'Look at you, you've ruined your clothes with all that climbing.'

She was angry. I ran and tried to hide but she wasn't playing around. She walked out into the yard and snapped a branch off a bush. Then she found me hiding behind the rainwater barrel. It all happened so fast my butt was stinging before I could run again.

Being beaten like that was normal in my culture. Everybody whipped their children to keep them in line. Most, like my parents, would only do it when they felt it was absolutely necessary. The teachers at school would do it too. It wasn't until I went to a school run by Italian nuns that I realised that not all adults whipped children.

That school was my favourite. Like so many of the good things in our town, it was operated by Christian missionaries from Europe rather than by the government. These people came from all over the world to help improve our lives, little by little. The world knew that the civil war had destroyed much of our country and had turned vast numbers into refugees, many of whom ended up in Wau with few prospects for the future. Aid organisations sent volunteers to help the people who were in need. Often they were missionaries who wanted to convert us to their religions, and many times they succeeded, which was why there are so many Christian Dinka. But some of the organisations didn't bother with God talk and just got on with simple plans to make things better. UNICEF did one of the best things ever seen in Wau when they built a series of well pumps across town. I'll forever be grateful for that clean water. I was lucky they built a pump near our house. Many people in the Sudan walk for hours every day to collect water, but we just had to go down the road.

As I got older, my mother started sending me to the pump for water every morning and evening, which I enjoyed. I had to stay at home after school, working or doing lessons, so going to the well was one of the few times I'd get to see my friends. We'd chat about things – our teachers, other kids – or play games. Once, when we were playing, I was thrown in the trough that collected the water and had to walk home soaking wet. My mother didn't like that.

More rarely I would be able to sneak off to a place that I loved. Near the well, a path led up across the grass to the highest part of town. Great spreading acacia trees shaded the trail and there were tall lulu trees on the hill. Sometimes I'd see women gathering the small lulu nuts. Later they would press the nuts to get shea butter, which is prized as a moisturiser. There, on the hill, I could see for miles across the vast plain that surrounded Wau. I'd sit in the grass and scan the horizon for aeroplanes coming in to land at the airport. The silver glint of sunlight hitting the wings would mesmerise me and I'd lose myself in imagining where the plane had been and what kind of people were on board. Well-dressed foreigners from somewhere far away, I knew. Farther than Khartoum. The other side of the world, perhaps. I loved my home town, my family and our house, but I also loved to imagine flying through the deep blue sky heading somewhere exciting.

I knew what that was like because when I was a little girl I flew in one of those planes, all by myself, when I was sent for medical treatment in Khartoum. I'd had serious psoriasis all over my body since I was baby. No one knew what to do about it. It made my entire body itch and I'd scratch my skin until it bled. Often it would get infected and ooze pus. There were scabs all over my legs, arms and chest, even on my face. The palms of my hands would get cracked and sore and it felt better to keep them closed so the wounds didn't stretch.

'Alek, open your hands,' my mother always said. 'If you keep them closed they're going to heal that way and you'll never get them open again.'

She hated seeing me suffer. When I felt like crying from the pain I would sneak off to a corner where she couldn't see me, because when she did she'd look like she was going to start crying too. I even had it on the bottoms of my feet and walking on the open sores just made it worse. Sometimes I could see the meaty part of my flesh through the cracks, and all the oozing liquid, and I'd feel so ashamed. But I just had to get used to it. My skin turned ashy and white. My mother shaved my head and rubbed Vaseline into my scalp to keep it from flaking away.

It's so strange that I grew up to make my living off my looks, after so many years of looking like a monster. I'm lucky we didn't have many mirrors.

My mother became desperate because nothing she did helped. She dressed me in my only good dress, a cotton shift with thin yellow and pink stripes and patch pockets, and we walked down to a little wooden storefront near the market. She rapped on the shutter that covered the window.

'Yes, one minute, please,' came the shopkeeper's voice.

This wasn't our usual store. The man opened the shutter and peered at us with bloodshot eyes. Behind him were narrow shelves lined with beer and liquor bottles. A plastic bucket full of matches was on the counter, along with a tin cup full of loose cigarettes.

'Give me six cigarettes and a small bottle of the cane liquor,' my mother said.

I was shocked.

'But you don't drink!' I said.

'And I don't smoke, either,' she replied.

'What's that for then?'

'No need for questions from a little girl called Alek. That little girl's always got questions. You'll find out in time.'

The shopkeeper wrapped the cigarettes in a piece of newspaper and then did the same with the bottle before handing them to my mother, who quickly hid them in her pocket.

We continued down the hill towards a part of Wau that I'd always been forbidden to go near. It was on the far side of the railway line, literally on the wrong side of the tracks. Country people lived there, often in houses made of mud or even just in tents of sticks and cloth. Children ran around naked in the dirt.

We came to a small farm, with yellow flowers growing off a vine along the fence and herbs in pots near the porch of a little wooden building.

'Here we are,' my mother said.

'What?'

'There's a man here who's going to look at your skin. He's got special powers.'

19

I felt so nervous my stomach got jumpy. Then I smelled the goats: that sour, stale, stomach-churning goat smell. I could see a herd of them and a bucket of goat's milk sat on a rock in the sun collecting flies. I wanted to throw up.

My mother called out.

'What do you want with me?' came a man's voice.

'I came with my daughter,' my mother said.

He opened the door and smoke from his cooking fire drifted out. Then he followed the smoke, looking like something out of a fairy tale. He had matted grey dreadlocks, a wispy beard with beads plaited into it and yellowish eyes. His raggedy clothes were held together with twine and he wore a necklace of feathers. I was sure he was crazy. Why was my mother bringing me here?

'Look at you,' he said, examining my forearm. 'You need help.'

He negotiated a price with my mother – she would bring him a sack of peanuts. The smell of animals and smoke was overpowering as we stepped into his dark house. Bright sunlight filtered through cracks in the plank walls.

'Tobacco?' he demanded.

My mother handed him the cigarettes and the bottle of cane liquor.

'Stand,' he said to me.

He took a handful of fresh herbs and shook them around my body while he mumbled supplications to God, or the Devil, who knew? Then he rubbed the herbs on my arms and face to release the oils, before scraping my skin with a thin wooden spatula. When he had finished he showed me a pile of granules that he said he'd scraped off my skin. They looked like rotten millet. It was disgusting and I knew it was all a trick. He gave me a strange look, as if he knew exactly what I was thinking. Then he took a swig of liquor and sprayed it out of his mouth in a fine mist to coat my skin. He opened the newspaper, took out a cigarette and examined the brand. He smiled. My mother had brought the counterfeit Marlboros, which were more expensive than the Sudanese brands. He lit the cigarette and blew short puffs of smoke in my face, making me cough. Then he inhaled a huge lungful of smoke, burning at least a quarter of the cigarette. He let the smoke out in a cloud and wafted his hands so it coated my body. 'Done,' he said. 'Wait outside.'

I stood in the yard, itching my skin like crazy, until my mother came out with a bag of herbs. All the way home I forced myself not to scratch because I didn't want my mother to think she'd wasted her time and money on this witch doctor. But I knew she had.

At home my mother steeped the herbs until they made a thick, bitter drink that made me gag. For two weeks I dreaded my morning dose of this concoction. Of course, it didn't help at all. My skin still bled and oozed and itched. She took me to several other healers, each of them weird and a bit scary, but none of them helped. I could see sadness and a sense of hopelessness on my mother's face.

Finally she decided I should go to Khartoum. My father was there getting treatment for a broken hip. He'd accidentally ridden his bicycle into a deep pothole one dark night on a road not far from our house. The doctors in Khartoum inserted steel pins into the bone to hold it together. My father was staying with my uncle, who was a doctor, and my brother Athian while he recuperated. My mother thought that if anyone could help me my uncle could. She also thought it would be good for me to visit my father. So, one morning she packed me a little bag with a change of clothes and we walked several miles out of town to the airport. There, she asked the flight attendants to look after me and I walked out onto the tarmac and climbed the stairs to the plane. The propellers looked massive; I had no doubt that they would be able to carry us aloft over the desert.

Inside, I sat in the most comfortable seat I'd ever known. I could see the pilot in the cockpit with all the complicated dials and buttons. It was exciting, but it was also hard to leave my mother. Looking out of the little window I saw her at the edge of the runway. I waved and waved but she never waved back. I guess she couldn't see me. We took off and flew high above the Nilotic plain to the city. Athian met me at the airport and I stayed in Khartoum for months, visiting doctors who all said my psoriasis was incurable. Finally my mother sent word that I should return home and go to school. Back in Wau my skin got even worse. We saw more witch doctors. Nothing helped. Later my mother somehow got me into a German missionary hospital over an hour's walk outside of town, near the Jur River. The Germans were known for being good with skin conditions so we thought they would be able to find a cure. I remember that on one of my first days there a German doctor took one look at me, said, 'Oh my God,' and left the room. It was that bad.

I stayed in that hospital for a month. They rubbed creams on my body and wrapped my legs and hands in bandages. It drove me mad not to be able to scratch but that helped me heal a little. The food was good and I rested in the sun. But I was so lonely by myself. My parents came to visit as often as they could, but it was too far for them to come every day. I

22

missed my mother so much. Sometimes she would stay at the hospital for a few days, but not often as she had to look after my brothers and sisters at home.

The hospital was like a maze, with rooms off a veranda and a hidden courtyard filled with flowers. It was really clean and pleasant. Eventually my skin healed and they said I could go home. I felt great. But as soon as I stopped the treatments the psoriasis came back and I started scratching myself until I bled. It was agony. I couldn't squeeze a lemon without my hands burning as the juice got into the cracks. The other children would sometimes make fun of me. I hated it. I didn't feel normal.

I think that the years I spent suffering from psoriasis taught me not to take beauty too seriously. Just looking at someone and passing judgement like that isn't really so meaningful – saying someone is ugly or beautiful. Beauty is a much deeper issue. I know, because I was ugly for much of my childhood, and then my skin cleared up and people thought just the opposite but I remained the same person, with an ugly side and a beautiful side like everyone else. There was nothing substantially different about me; my skin was just better.

Despite my psoriasis, I had a pretty good childhood. Often in the mornings, if I wasn't at school, I'd go to the market with my mother to get vegetables and meat from the women who brought their supplies in from the countryside on donkeys. The meat could be really nasty, because they just cut it up and laid it out on tables in the open air, with flies buzzing on it. You had to cook it thoroughly to kill any parasites. There wasn't any choice, so we didn't really think about it very much. You could find anything at the market, even fat roasted termites that people would crunch between their teeth like potato crisps.

One of my favourite foods was a flatbread called *kissra*. To prepare it you make a batter from corn or other grains, pour it out onto a griddle and then spread the batter out with a palm leaf. When it's done you lift it off the griddle and stack it on top of the others you've cooked, like American pancakes. The bread is dipped into stews.

There was a stew called *Ni'aimiya*, made of onions, spices, peanuts and okra or meat, sometimes with yogurt or milk mixed in. There were other stews that I liked even more, called *waika*, *bussaara* and *sabaroag*, which were made from dried okra powder and sometimes had potatoes, aubergines and spices in them. Our main, day-to-day food was a wheat or corn porridge called *asseeda*. Sometimes my mother would serve the porridge with a dried fish dish called *kajaik*.

For a special feast, we might also have *elmaraara* or *umfitit*, which are made from sheep offal, onions, peanut butter and salt and eaten raw. I loved the rare occasions when we had soups such as *kawar'i*, made of cattle hoofs and vegetables, and *elmussalammiya*, which is made from liver, flour, dates and spices. We mostly drank tea or water, and possibly milk. Every once in a while we'd have fruit drinks, which were made by blending orange and lemon pulp with water.

My mother tells me that I had my own special diet when I was a young girl: I liked to eat sand.

'I'd find you licking it off the walls,' she said. 'I'd always be catching you putting sand in your mouth.'

She thought the sand had caused my psoriasis, but I doubt it. I don't know why I ate sand. I know that some people eat dirt and scientists say it's a way for them to get the minerals they need. I can't really imagine it, but perhaps I was missing something in my diet. Who knows? I felt it was a completely normal childhood. Until the tanks came. When I was nine, great rumbling convoys of army trucks draped with soldiers entered Wau. Everything changed.

CHAPTER 2

It was shocking to hear army trucks rumbling through the streets of my little town and to see men in green uniforms leaning against the walls of my friends' houses. Wau was not my simple home any longer; it was a military zone, with rebels on the outskirts, soldiers in town and the lawless militias wreaking havoc everywhere. I couldn't even climb the hill to spot planes any more, because the soldiers had communications equipment up there and they'd be suspicious of what a young Dinka girl was doing.

For several months only military flights had been allowed to land at the airport so I'd known that a lot of soldiers were coming into the area. They'd kept pretty much to themselves and I'd hardly seen them on the streets. Now I couldn't walk to school without passing lots of guns, and even tanks. I marvelled at the machinery. It was hard to imagine they could turn it on me, but when my mother told us never to dawdle on the streets because they were just too dangerous I began to realise that the soldiers weren't necessarily there to protect me. My parents definitely didn't allow us out after dark.

However, we tried to keep our daily activities up. My mother would still take the cows to pasture and there was always water to bring home from the pump. One afternoon my younger sister Athieng and I put our plastic water containers on our heads and went to fetch water. We saw some other children there and we started playing hide-and-seek. I loved hanging out with Athieng because, unlike my other siblings, she didn't boss me around. She actually looked up to me.

I was in my favourite hiding place, behind a fat old acacia tree – for some reason everyone always forgot to look there. After a while we paused for a drink of water. Suddenly the daylight turned that deep yellow colour you only see on the equator and I realised that twilight was descending. Mother would be worried.

'We've got to get home,' I said, grabbing Athieng's arm. We filled the canisters and rushed off, droplets falling onto our faces as we hadn't closed the lids properly. I made sure my sister kept her eyes on the path whenever we met someone on the way home. The darkness always made the militias hungry for stealing and shooting. I wasn't going to let anyone hurt my sister.

A green military half-track passed, kicking up red dust. One of the soldiers in camouflage peered at me from below his dark beret. His teeth were white and he licked his dry lips as he watched us.

We ran back along the road, passing more green trucks on the way. Helmets, guns and gas canisters hung from the sides of the trucks and the soldiers looked primed, excited, ready for action. It scared the life out of me. My sister and I ran into our courtyard and hurriedly closed the gate, trying to keep the world out. There were our mother's cows, her vegetables. It felt good to be home.

Inside, my mother and father were hunched over the radio, listening at low volume. My mother looked up, held her finger in front of her mouth and said, 'Shhhh – close the door.'

They were listening to the rebel radio station, which was illegal. You didn't want anyone to catch you listening to it. On the radio the announcer was saying that the conflict had spread to Wau.

'War?' I said.

My father nodded. The war had resumed, after ten years of peace. They'd been keeping it from us children, hoping that it would bypass Wau. But now it was too late for that.

The second civil war began in 1983, when I was six years old, after the rebel leader John Garang formed the Sudan People's Liberation Army (SPLA) to fight off the northern troops that were trying to dominate the south. Fanatical conservative Muslims were threatening President Gaafar Nimeiry's rule and he decided that he couldn't let the south be autonomous any longer.

Gaafar Nimeiry announced that the whole of my country would henceforth become an Arab Muslim land. The north was hit first. He declared a state of emergency in that part of the country and suspended most of the constitution, replacing northern courts with special 'emergency courts' run according to shariah. Shariah is a system by which Muslim clerics can interpret the Koran and Muslim teachings to decide how people should live. It's often called the 'Islamic law' and can be very harsh, with amputations and stonings being used to punish people for adultery or selling liquor. Non-Muslims were given fewer rights and, along with women, were considered second-class citizens. But there was no way around it – this was the new law.

It wasn't long before we started hearing that one-handed thieves were walking shame-faced on the streets of Khartoum, their hand having been removed as punishment for their crime. A money trader there was hanged for having non-Sudanese bills in his pocket. Entrepreneurial women were whipped for selling alcohol. Opposition leaders were jailed. Fearing Nimeiry's attempts to impose shariah on the south, and not wanting to be dominated in any way by the north, the SPLA fought back. Towns and villages began to fall to the rebels all across the south. Each time the rebels won a battle their radio station would play a special song. Wau was a prime target for both sides because of its airport.

Almost overnight, my parents became much more protective of us. Wau had always been a trading crossroads where Dinka, Blanda, Nual, Shual, Muslims, Christians and others all lived together happily. I always found it interesting to learn about other people's customs and traditions. Us Dinka have ceremonial marriages to cows. Other tribes marry goats.

Once the soldiers arrived the easy social life we had with our neighbours from different tribes and religions fell apart. Everyone became suspicious of other people. Suddenly, we heard some of our neighbours saying it was the Dinka who were causing all the trouble. That if it weren't for the Dinka, who made up a lot of the rebel SPLA, there would still be peace. In the Sudan it's generally very easy for a person to tell which tribe you're from, just by the way you look or dress. For instance, the Gurchol men wore bands of string around their waists and draped cloth from the front down between their legs and up the back, where it was again tucked into the band so that the end draped over. The various types of Dinka were easily distinguished, not only by their tall, thin bodies but by the dotted or v-shaped scars on their foreheads and cheeks.

These accusations about the Dinka made us fear that we'd be singled out.

It was the dry season and the nights were really hot. We loved spreading blankets out on the veranda or on the ground in the evening so we could lie in the cooler night air and tell each other stories until we fell asleep. We always went to sleep really early because we knew the neighbourhood chickens and dogs would wake us before sunrise, or earlier. Suddenly our parents said we couldn't sleep outside any more because of the fighting on the outskirts of town.

We started locking the doors to the house in the early evening and if one of us was out when the sun started setting, at seven or so, we'd panic.

'Where's Deng? Where's Athieng? It's getting dark!' my mother would say of my younger brother and sister. 'I hope they don't run into *those* people.'

All through my childhood I'd felt safe in Wau but it was now clear that even the local police had no real control. We kept hearing about militias that were forming, groups of gang-sters with no political loyalties at all. They were dispossessed men who had been run out of their home towns by the government soldiers, they were poor or they were just bad seeds. All they wanted was to rob, molest, rape and destroy. They didn't care who you were. Out in the countryside they would break into a farm, killing the owners and stealing all their food. That's how they got their provisions. Many of them weren't much more than teenagers with guns. Sometimes they would kill a policeman and steal his uniform, so you never really knew who you could trust.

They were the darkness people, only coming out at night, so I hardly ever saw them.

One evening I was lying on my bed when I heard some men outside in the street, yelling like they were drunk.

'Mother!' I cried out. 'What's that?'

'Hush,' she said harshly.

I hushed.

'It's militia,' she whispered. 'We can't let them know we're here.'

We huddled in silence, fearing the worst. Then we heard them pass.

My friend Aisha told me stories about the militias stealing children from their families and selling them as slaves. She said that there were slave corrals out in the bush where the child slaves got water only once a day and stale bread with meal worms in it just twice a week, if they were lucky. My world suddenly seemed perilous.

Some of our neighbours disappeared. We never saw them moving out of their houses or walking away. We just noticed that they had gone. We would hear gunshots in the night and then the rumours would come down to our yard, passed over the walls, from wife to wife. The whispers were terrifying: 'Did you hear what happened to Robert? He's gone. Dead.' Or 'Deng's wife was kidnapped at gunpoint and taken away to be a slave.'

One afternoon the radio announcer said, matter-of-factly, that everyone in Wau should stay in their houses because a rebel offensive was just beginning. The rebels wanted to take control of the town and its airport. Since they were mostly Dinka it was quite confusing, we didn't know which side to trust – our government or our people?

My father's view was more along the lines of 'Dinka or not Dinka, they could easily kill you. Let's not get too excited about the rebels coming to liberate Wau.' He didn't trust any of them.

The sound of Kalashnikovs peppered most nights and I never got used to it, I could never sleep through it. The rebels were fighting the army. The army was fighting the police. The gangsters were killing whoever stood between them and money, or clothes, chickens or even someone's old flip-flops. You couldn't turn your head without seeing an automatic rifle. If there was a bullet to spare, it might just be for you. The sound of the weapons went into me as surely as any bullet.

Every day we ran home from school and closed the gate tightly, trying to keep out the impending darkness. My mother sometimes scolded us out of sheer worry, then gave us a hug.

'You stay inside now,' she would say.

She served us a meal of *kissra*, and okra stew. Then we heard men coming up the road, just on the other side of our wall. They shouted at a man and we heard him pleading with them for mercy. They gave it. They laughed at him and they let him go. Then they went on to harass or kill their next victim, depending on their mood. These militias were our nightmare.

We crowded around the radio whenever we could, addicted to the war news. We'd hear that another city had fallen to the rebels. It was hard to believe because the government soldiers were definitely keeping the rebels from entering Wau, although we'd heard that there were plenty of them on the outskirts of town. More soldiers poured into town each day.

32

We'd hear the trucks, hear their ammo going off at night as they chased down militia or fired weapons at random around the town.

One morning I was walking to school when a convoy of trucks started moving into the centre of town. I stood next to a tree and watched the procession pass. It was a long line of them, grinding into town, like nothing that we'd seen so far in the war. The government was really gearing up for something. It made me think that maybe these rebels were a bigger deal than I thought. Perhaps there was a good reason for the rebels being so powerful they could scare the government. Maybe the rebels had some good points. But I wished it would all end.

Having all these government soldiers in Wau gave it the feel of a military compound. Everything seemed so unfriendly. I could tell that my parents were nervous. I started worrying that they might be killed or kidnapped, or just disappear. If you start to think about your mum or dad disappearing, I mean, that's a scary shadow to have over you when you're just nine years old. I had felt free until the troops arrived. I began to think that the government must have been doing something very wrong if they had to back it up with all this force.

Still, despite the war, we needed water every day.

To carry the water we used old cooking oil containers that you could buy in the market. I would coil a piece of cloth on top of my head, set the container up there and then head off.

'You're skinny but your neck is strong,' I remember my sister telling me one day.

'It's all in your heart, you know,' I replied. 'It doesn't matter how big your muscles are.'

With that empty canister on my head I'd turn right out of

the gate and walk up the dirt road. Most of our neighbours lived in modest cement-block or wood houses, some of them quite makeshift. There was one mansion, with porches all around and brick walls. It was the home of a man who owned a large brewery on the edge of town, near the river. There were so few rich people in Wau we never thought of the differences between them and us, but we knew they had more possessions. While I wasn't jealous or covetous, I loved imagining myself living in that house, with its upholstered furniture and electricity generator. Just past this mansion — which, in truth, was probably no larger than the average middle-class English house in the London suburbs — was a road that went left up the hill to where I had once spotted planes. To the right it descended into a poor area, where some of the militias came from. By poor, I mean that people were barely able to cobble homes together from scrap wood and straw, and rarely had more than a couple of days' worth of food in the house at any time.

'Don't ever go down there by yourself,' my father had warned me. 'Someone might want to kill you.'

The police were always down there, fighting with the militias.

The well pump was right at this junction, in a broad field of green grass that was as beautiful to me as any park I've seen since. One day, when we went there, everyone had gone, except my sister Adaw and me. I smelled something awful in the air. I knew it was death. Then I saw a woman's body lying in the grass about fifty yards away, her tongue hanging out like an old piece of leather. She couldn't have been there very long but already her corpse smelled rotten, owing to the intense heat. I wanted to see her corpse up close.

'No Alek, don't!' Adaw said.

I realised she was right. Then I saw another body. We ran straight home.

After that my mother would always come with us to get water and it wasn't at all unusual to see dead bodies there.

'Don't look,' my mother would say.

How could we help it? I sneaked glances on every visit we made to the pump. Over time the bodies turned into bones, bones inside clothes. That was war to me – dead bodies left to rot.

If my mother could have carried enough water on her head for all of us she would have gone to the pump by herself. The killing field at the pump got worse every week. I worried that the rotting bodies were going to seep into the water supply, but my mother said that they were too far away. Still, every time I took a sip of water I thought of those bones.

Soon my mother forbade us from leaving the house alone. She didn't need to worry. I was too scared to leave. I was going to stay safe inside our house for ever, my mother always near. Before the war, in the evenings us children walked by ourselves to the missionary school to play volleyball and other games. That seemed absurd now. The nuns cancelled everything so that they could stay in the safety of their convent. My parents made sure we were inside, behind the gate, by five o'clock.

Word was that the local police were running out of ammunition. They had always done their best to protect the local people but now the only ones with bullets in our town were the government soldiers who, when it came down to it, really couldn't care less about people like us, especially the Dinka, and the gangster militias, who definitely didn't care about anyone. Those two groups just started shooting at each other all over town. All night long there'd be Katyusha rockets blazing across the sky, and the sound of automatic weapons being fired and men yelling. I always woke before dawn and that was the only quiet hour. We couldn't leave our courtyard. The shooting got so bad that, at one point, we couldn't leave our house for three days. Strangely, all the violence led to a kind of beautiful togetherness in the neighbourhood. My mother had stockpiled some potatoes and other roots; we had enough dried okra to last, and several containers of water. Our neighbours had done the same. If someone needed something they would just ask their neighbour for help. I remember passing a bucket of milk over the wall to the woman next door. In turn, she got some tomatoes. We took care of each other.

Just before sunset on the second night my family shared a meal of *kissra* and okra stew. After we had cleared everything away my older brother Mayen helped our father get to his feet so he could use the latrine in the courtyard. He had come back from Khartoum with the pins still in his left hip to help it heal. The doctors had told him to come back to have them removed and he had planned to, but then things in Wau became very difficult. His hip became badly infected and he could only hobble. With such trouble walking, he fell and broke his left arm too. He was having a miserable time but there was no way he could return to Khartoum for treatment. He struggled to get to the latrine each night, but he did it on his own. He was proud that way. I was worried for him.

There were a lot of trucks on the roads, and gunfire in the distance. For some reason everything felt even crazier than usual.

Then I heard men coming up the road. Some trucks. All of a sudden a fire-fight broke out right outside our house, just as my father was struggling to get back from the latrine – he was having a hard time walking because of his bad hip. He had to throw himself to the ground to avoid the bullets flying over the wall. My heart ached to watch him lying in the dirt, his face racked with agony. We couldn't do anything for him.

'Duck! Duck!' my mother instructed him.

The bullets kept flying. That was the longest twenty minutes of my life.

In the morning my parents whispered to each other, and their faces seemed more worried than ever. The radio said that all citizens of Wau should prepare to evacuate.

Then that night a group of militias appeared at our wall and pounded on the metal gate. My mother gave my father a worried look.

We had no idea who they were or what they were looking for.

'They must be at the wrong house,' said my mother.

They started fiddling with the lock on the gate.

'Hush,' my mother said. 'They can't know we're here.'

She blew out the kerosene lantern and we huddled together in terrified silence.

Just then the militias got through our front gate. I could hear them walking outside near the veranda, moving very carefully. By that time so many civilians had taken up arms that the militias were afraid of being shot by us.

My mother suddenly sat up with a jolt and said, 'I left the front door unlocked.'

She crept to the door and flicked the latch. The lock made a clicking, metallic sound. The militias' guns exploded in a blast of bullets. They must have thought the clicking lock was a gun. They sprayed bullets into our walls and through our windows. We dived under the beds to hide, but my father couldn't bend well enough and his legs were sticking out. He was almost crying from pain. Then the shooting stopped. The militias fled. They must have thought we were shooting back at them, but we had no guns. Just an angel, I guess. We huddled together even as they left in search of easier prey. It felt like the darkest night ever.

CHAPTER 3

I stared into the darkness after the gunmen left. There was no moon and we couldn't light the oil lanterns for fear of the light being seen outside so it was impossible to see a thing. My little sister snored and fidgeted on the floor next to me, oblivious to everything. Gunfire in the distance kept me on edge, I feared the militias would return. There was a smell of gunpowder. Men were yelling. Each time one of the cows snorted out in the yard I thought it was someone climbing over the wall. Sucking in my stomach and flattening my shoulders to the cold concrete floor made me as thin as a board. The bullets, if they came, would whizz right above me.

It's the same thing I do now on the runway – throw my shoulders back and lengthen my body. In ten years I went from dodging bullets in a scarred and frightened little town to strutting for fashion editors while wearing elaborate couture.

But that night I had no dreams of Paris, no ideas about

London, no clue as to where exactly New York was. Not even a hint that I was about to become a refugee myself.

The rebels and the government both wanted control of the airport in Wau so they were going at it with guns, bombs, clubs and whatever else they could muster. If my family got caught in the middle we'd all be killed. The militias were the most terrifying of all. They would move down the dirt streets blasting Michael Jackson's 'Thriller' from a stereo while they robbed anyone who got in their way. They would steal a family's cooking pots. They would shoot people on their way to market and take the few coins they had set aside for food. A lot of the militias were still children.

As I waited for sunrise I pictured the soldiers, the rebels and the militias attacking each other. I had seen dead bodies so I knew what happened when someone got shot. In my imagination they shot and stabbed and kicked each other until they were all dead and we were able to sleep in peace.

Still sleep didn't come so I drifted between prayer and imagination, just trying to keep my mind off what was happening outside. I thought of a photo I saw in a magazine that a foreign aid worker had left behind at my school. It was of an ochre-coloured house in a grove of tall pine trees on the edge of the sea somewhere far from Africa. The dining room had high glass walls; the table was set for a big meal and decorated with a huge vase of sunflowers. The light in that photo was a soft yellow and it felt so peaceful. I wondered if people really lived like that, or if it was just a fantasy.

The shrill sound of 122 mm Katyusha rockets made me jump. What if a rocket came right through the roof, right into our room? I had to pee but I held it in. It got painful but I wasn't about to step outside after what had happened to

40

my father. More Katyushas went off, closer this time, and when they exploded I swear the ground shook. Then there was utter silence, even more frightening than the sound of the rockets. I was sure we were going to die.

Somehow I was so tired that somewhere between that thought and the roosters crowing, I dozed off. When I woke up, the air smelled of death. I wanted to vomit. Then my mother walked into the room.

'Alek, what are you dreaming about? It's time to get up,' she said.

She stood over me and my sisters, stirring the air over our heads with a 'wush wush wush' of her hands. That meant, 'Get moving, girls!'

I opened the door to the early morning sunlight. For a moment the world looked lovely. Our neighbour's banana tree rustled in the breeze and a palm stood tall against the coming light. My mother's cows had lined up in the courtyard as usual, waiting for her to lead them out to the pasture.

Meanwhile, my father stirred on his bed, taking his time getting up. He was only in his fifties but he moved like an old man. His hip was killing him after sleeping all night on the floor but he didn't make a sound as he slowly uncurled to his full height. He just stretched, said 'good morning', and turned on his radio. He usually listened to the BBC, but sometimes in the afternoon he'd turn on the rebel radio station, very softly, so the government soldiers wouldn't hear it and haul him away. My family didn't really get involved in politics. Since the rebels of the SPLA were mostly from the south, where we lived, and were mostly Dinka, like us, they treated us pretty fairly. My parents were probably more inclined to support them but as a family we tried to stay out

41

of the way of anyone with a gun. There wasn't much profit in taking sides.

The radio said that the local government was urging all the people of Wau to flee. The situation was just too dangerous.

'As if we didn't know,' said my mother.

I held the hem of my dress, as if to protect myself, and stepped gingerly into the yard with my sister. Everything looked calm so we went to the gate and looked outside. People were already walking down the road carrying loads on their heads. The exodus had begun. Then my sister beckoned me over to see some bullet holes that had splintered the wood of our gate that was sheathed in zinc.

'Mama, look at this,' we called out.

My mother came over and shook her head. Then she pointed to a hole in the ground where one of the militiamen had rested his rifle. 'Bayonet,' was all she said.

Back inside my parents huddled in private. This was how they always did it. They talked things over and came to an agreement. It's really quite inspiring to remember how my mother and father were able to communicate so well and work together to face all the hardships that they had suffered.

At one point I heard my mother say, 'That's it – I can't take this any more.' Then she saw that I was listening and lowered her voice. When their conversation ended my father turned to us. His skin was pale but his eyes were on fire.

'We will leave for the villages today. It's no longer safe for us here.'

From the tone of his voice we knew that we had no choice.

My parents had spent their entire childhoods in the midst of various wars in the Sudan. Ever since the British colonialists granted my country independence in 1956, we've been ruled by military regimes that backed Islamic governments, although the country – the largest in Africa – is made up of a lot of different tribes and religions. Finding a common centre has been tough. When they were growing up, and also after they started a family, my parents had to flee their homes for nearby countries such as Congo, Uganda and the Central African Republic.

None of this was new to my parents. They were about to be refugees again. If it made them sad, they never showed it.

The villages where my parents and their extended families had grown up were south of Wau, far from the main roads. In the villages people still lived in the old ways, in round mud huts with no running water. They grew or hunted almost all their food and in the dry season the younger people would take the cattle far from the villages, to an oasis, and lived there while the cattle grazed. The villages had no telephones so it was hard to get information from our relatives about how things were going in the countryside. My parents thought that if we went to one of these villages we might be safe. There was no guarantee so we just had to walk there and take our chances.

I had never been that far into the countryside and I had no idea what lay in front of us. I'd heard that things down there could be really strange. On the few times our cousins had come up to Wau to visit us they'd worn makeshift clothes, and sometimes they had fleas or lice that they would ask us to pick out of their hair. All my friends would tease them. My aunts would sit in bed with their shoes on, getting dirt all over the sheets, which we thought was quite peculiar. But my father said that's how they did it at home, where they slept on straw mats instead of beds.

Years later, when I went to England, I got a first hand lesson in how wrong it is to judge people by their backgrounds. That's because I was misjudged myself. In Wau I belonged to a well-educated, sophisticated family but in London I was the one everyone teased for being a primitive country girl.

In their eyes I was no different from my village cousins. I was an unsophisticated African whose skin was darker than night. They were second or third generation immigrants, with lighter skin, and they knew the ways of London. I realised then that it is all relative, and that you shouldn't think badly of others for not having the same advantages or viewpoint. I felt bad for having judged my village cousins harshly at times in the past. In fact, I felt like I would have given anything just to see their friendly faces at that moment. It had taken a long journey for me to figure this out.

After we had a quick cup of tea my mother started 'packing' for the trip. She didn't haul suitcases out of the closet as I would do today. She didn't tell us to fold our underwear and get three changes of clothes, or pack all our toiletries in a bag. No, none of that. Instead, she laid sheets on the ground, which would be wrapped up around everything. She told me which cooking pot to grab from the kitchen. We took a knife, one or two cups and a container for water. All eight of us would be eating with our fingers in the Dinka way so there was no need for many utensils. My mother packed powdered okra that she could cook along the way, since there would be nowhere to get food. She carefully tied up a bundle of salt, for cooking and trading with people. It was worth a lot because outside of the towns people rarely had salt. We gathered all this up into the sheets that would serve as our suitcases.

These days, when I travel I have maid service, room service, laundry service and turn-down service. Back then, we had nothing really, bar our wits. The amazing thing was that my parents made us feel safe and comfortable anyway. Which just goes to show that comfort is a state of mind.

I was comfortable that morning in my nicest outfit, a flower print cotton dress with an elastic waist that we had bought in the market. It was very simple. That and flip-flops was all I wore. None of us took even a change of clothes or waterproofs or anything personal.

Before we could leave my mother had to say goodbye to her cattle. They were her children in a way. Each one had a name and she could pick out their faces from far away. Cattle have always been central to the Dinka culture and are part of our identity. One of our myths is that when our god, called Nhialac, created the Dinka he gave us a choice between having cattle or a mysterious unknown something he called the 'what'. The Dinka chose cattle because they represented wealth and dignity. That has given us Dinka a very strong self-image, which has been passed down through the generations. I know this has helped me remain positive through all the difficulties I've faced in my life. As a Dinka woman, I've always been proud that my ancestors were smart enough to choose the cattle over the 'what'.

These days, with all the Dinka people who have moved abroad, the culture has begun to change. We see a lot of other kinds of wealth that we never saw in the southern Sudan, ranging from the average Londoner's reliable plumbing to celebrities' sports cars, and we realise that living in the old ways isn't necessarily such a rich life after all. Still, we try to keep our culture intact. Cattle remain symbolically important to me and other Sudanese expatriates, even if it's not very practical to keep livestock in our new homes far from Africa in places like London, New York and Sydney.

When I think about all that has been destroyed and changed by the war I am inspired by a quote from Ariathdit, an early twentieth century Dinka prophet. At the turn of the century the British colonialists put him in prison for sedition while they took over the country. After they released him he said, 'Piny nhom abi riak mac.' Which means, 'The land may be spoiled, yet it will remain intact.' We may have lost a great deal during the civil war but the Dinka culture will never be destroyed.

That's how my mother always thought. That's what led her to arrange in advance for a local man to drive her herd of cattle down to the village if the time ever came that we had to flee. She would preserve our family culture even if everything else about us had to change. The cattle would be really valuable in the village. We could get milk from them, or could even sell one if we had to. They would also give us a sense of self-worth and a spiritual connection to our past.

The morning we left our home my mother was able to say goodbye to her cattle in peace because she knew she'd see them soon. Even though we were in a rush to get as far from the fighting as possible before nightfall she spoke softly to each cow by name, giving this one a scratch and that one a rub, assuring each one that everything was going to be fine. I swear they gave her sympathetic looks in return. If I hadn't been so sure that my mother loved me even more than she loved her cows, I would have been jealous. I don't think she'd ever have been able to flee Wau without knowing that her cattle would be cared for, and that she'd see them soon.

Walking out through the front gate I felt sad to leave our home behind. Most of us children were pretty young at the time. I was just nine, and then there was Mayen, eighteen, the joker of the family, Adaw, fourteen, who definitely always acted like my 'older sister', Akuol, twelve, who was serious and sensitive and very loving – we were quite close – Athieng, seven, who idolised me in the way that little sisters do, and little Deng who, at only four, was the baby of the family, the little king. The three other siblings, who were older, were away studying and working.

It was going to be hard for us to walk far but we all carried something, however small, on our heads for a little bit of time. Even Deng knew that when we weren't carrying him he'd have to carry a little bundle himself. There was no choice and even as children we knew that if we stayed in Wau we would probably be killed.

I balanced one of the smaller bundles on my head and stepped out into the road with the rest of my family. People sometimes called us the Wek Army because there were so many of us. That's what kept us together and helped us do so well: we were a little community of our own, my mother and father, my brothers and sisters.

It was a hot morning and the mist burned off quickly as we walked along the road, which was already busy with other people fleeing their homes. The main road out of town was packed with people, as if a whole city had come together to form an endless line of refugees. We were those very images you see sometimes on the television. A couple of years ago I was in the first class lounge at JFK waiting for a flight to Paris when CNN started showing footage of people fleeing their homes in Sierra Leone. It was a long line of dark-skinned people, mothers holding children's hands, fathers carrying bundles, the lucky ones wearing sandals and the rest barefoot on the dusty road. Looking around me at all the well-dressed, well-fed people chatting into their phones or pressing buttons on their electronic gadgets in the lounge I suddenly felt very much alone. In many ways I felt closer to these refugees in their ragged clothes than I did to the privileged international travellers whose class I had somehow joined.

That morning in Wau I was right in the middle of it, heading off into the bush, to a world I'd never seen before. There were all kinds of people on the road: Muslim women covered in deep red, or blue or green scarves, Nubian men in long white robes, Christians wearing American cast-offs from the markets. But mostly it was Dinka like us who were walking south, towards the borders with Uganda and Zaïre. We were headed deep into Dinka territory, where our ancestors had herded cattle for untold generations.

As the miles passed the crowd of people on the road thinned out, as some families veered off toward their own ancestral lands, and by the time we reached the old brewery that produced all the beer for this part of the country the walk began to seem less stressful. The brewery sat on a huge plot near the Jur River, and over the years my mother had leased some of the property there to grow peanuts, which did well in the sandy soil. She sold the peanuts to get money for the family. Since they were friends, my parents walked over to chat with the manager. He was a tall, charcoal-skinned man, and I remember that he was very warm to my parents.

'Aren't you going to leave?' my father asked him.

'I can't,' he said. 'I've got to take care of the brewery.'

My mother shook her head.

'Don't be loyal to a fault,' she said. 'It's just bricks and beer when it comes down to it.'

'Well I won't risk my life for the bricks – but beer, that's another story!'

He was so good-natured, even in the face of it all. Before we left he gave my father some advice on which trail to follow. He said that once we had crossed the river we would have to avoid all roads as they were crawling with armed men, both rebels and militias.

'Stick to the bush,' he told us. 'You can't trust anybody.'

Just past the brewery, the pastureland at the sides of the road turned into wetlands, with tall reeds stretching out as far as we could see. There were only a few trees here and there – I'd never seen anything like this. Soon we reached the Jur River. Since it was the rainy season the river was high on the banks. It seemed so wide that I couldn't imagine what was on the other side. The river alone was terrifying. Everyone knew that in places it teemed with crocodiles and hippopotamuses and other animals, though my father assured us that there weren't any around here. I'd seen the huge fish that came out of these waters for sale in the market and I didn't want anything to do with them.

Some men had pulled their dugout canoes up onto the mud bank and there were probably two dozen people there waiting to cross. Out on the water I could see another dozen or so of these dugouts dangerously full of people and their possessions – including chickens, a goat or two, some big sacks of grain – bobbing up and down in the water. I was worried, as I'd never been swimming in my life.

In fact, I only learned to swim a few years ago, when I was twenty-seven. I was on a friend's yacht off the coast of Sardinia and, looking at that amazing sea, I said, 'Yes, I want to learn how to swim.' I was on vacation, surrounded by luxury, yet my first thought was that if I ever had to cross a river again I'd want to know how to swim! I got one of my friends to teach me. The first time I tried I sank like a stone, which terrified me, but I went back in. It was so beautiful, and so frustrating. I kept it up and after a few days I was floating on my back in the sea. It was the most amazing feeling – pure freedom. In a way, it let me conquer that river back in the Sudan, at least in my mind.

I had none of these thoughts at the river that day. Instead, I felt trapped. I knew I was going to drown.

'I'm not going,' I said to my mother.

She hardened her face and dropped her eyelids. As stubborn as I was, I couldn't stand up to The Look.

'If you want to live you'll get in that boat.'

I climbed into one of the canoes with three of my siblings. The captain looked scared and kept glancing nervously at the shore for men with guns. Nobody knew when the bullets would start flying. I sat in the front, back to back with my sister and our stuff was piled up around us. The boat wobbled as we set off and I yelled 'Help!', but my mother just said, 'Alek, hush.' I clutched the sides of that rough little boat so tightly I'm surprised they didn't snap. Luckily the water was calm that day.

Ironically, as we crossed the river we could see a perfectly good bridge upstream, but the government troops wouldn't let refugees like us use it. They wanted it closed in order to keep the rebels out. When we reached the other side I scampered out of the canoe and started walking.

The trail ran through high reeds so you couldn't see more

than a few feet in front of you. It was a tunnel of bright green grass and the ground was squishy and wet. My flip-flops kept catching on roots but my mother moved me along with her gentle encouragement.

By late afternoon we were still walking through the wetlands, surrounded by thick scrub and reeds. We could have just been wandering in circles, for all I knew: one bunch of shrubs looked pretty much like another. For my mother, the angle of the sun in the sky and the types of leaves on the bushes – one area has certain plants that another doesn't – were as good as any map. She had learned these tricks when she was young and, despite all our troubles, she found joy in walking through the bush.

'This is my childhood all over again,' she said.

Instead of acting like a hard-done-by mother of nine children she took the attitude of trying to teach us what she knew. Her good mood was infectious.

We hadn't eaten anything since our cup of tea that morning and were getting hungry. My mother spotted a bunch of pumpkin leaf growing nearby and sent me to collect it.

'Remember that, Alek?' she said. 'We bought it in the market.'

I did. I remembered the stew she made with the leaves, which made me even hungrier. We stopped a few more times along the trail to gather greens called tamalaca, as well as wild okra and a fruit called amaco ding. I was so hungry I wanted to eat it right there. Suddenly, my mother stopped dead in her tracks. There, not fifty yards away, were some SPLA rebels carrying weapons. Her face grew stony, which meant she was nervous. That made me afraid. The men had already spotted us and they came forward.

51

'Don't say a word,' my mother told us.

My father was a few hundred yards behind, walking slowly with Deng and Athieng, so he couldn't help.

My mother pressed her lips together, her face determined. I could see she was scared but I think what the men saw was a tough woman they wouldn't want to mess with. They were cold and businesslike, looking us up and down and examining our bundles of grain and cooking pots. My insides felt like jelly.

'You from Wau?' said one.

He looked like the leader, though he was dressed only in a ratty T-shirt, trousers and sneakers.

My mother said we were headed for the villages. He just grunted and stared. It looked like trouble to me.

Then, out of the blue, my mother surprised him with a big smile that melted his harsh face.

'Do you need anything?' she asked.

The soldier looked at her for a long moment that made me think that yes, he needed a lot, and that he wished we had more to give him. He needed guns and food and clothes and trucks and radios. He needed the government to stop trying to enforce Islam. He needed freedom for all the people in the Sudan.

'What do you have?' he asked.

'Soap,' said my mother. 'I could give you a bar of soap.'

He nodded. He had so little that a bar of soap was good enough. This was the kind of man the rebels thought could bring down the government? They had a few bullets but no food.

My father came up and after a tense moment he and the man shook hands. The other rebels watched. My parents spoke to the man for a while, gesturing up the trail. It looked like the man was giving them advice. The rebels left, fading into the bushes as silently as they'd appeared. Then my parents gathered us around and told us we weren't going to our father's village after all. The rebels had warned them there were some government troops in that direction. We were going to a different village instead, one where my father's more distant relatives lived.

'We don't know them but they'll welcome us,' my father assured us. 'We'll have a good life there.'

I had my doubts, but I didn't say so. Already it felt like we'd left any chance for a good life behind in Wau, but there was nothing to do but move forward.

We walked on, looking for a place to spend the night, until we finally found an abandoned hut.

'The animals won't come near a place where people have lived,' said my father.

We didn't break in, because that wouldn't be right. Instead, we swept the ground outside the hut with leafy branches to make a hard surface. Then we lay our mat on the dirt while my mother beat the ground with a big stick to let any wild animals in the area know that we were here and that we were human and that they'd better stay the heck away.

'But what about the snakes?' I said.

I hated snakes.

'The snakes don't want to eat little Alek,' my father said.

'And the lions?' I asked.

'Lions want a fat girl, not a skinny little girl like you,' he said. 'This is where we are so this is where we're staying.'

He was right. Where else were we going to go?

My mother sent us children off into the bush to look for dry wood and grass to build a fire, and told us that whoever brought back the most wood would win. She was always setting up games for us so everything, no matter how bad, would seem like fun. We found a little pond and brought back some water. My mother cooked the greens up into a stew, seasoned with a little salt, and cooked some grain to go with it. She boiled the water for us to drink. We gathered on the ground around our feast and ate it with our fingers from the three flowered enamel plates my mother had brought with us. Those plates made the meals so much nicer. It's amazing what a small amount of civility will do for you when you're in a hard situation.

We were so hungry this food tasted as good as any meal I'd ever had, though it was finished pretty quickly – there was only just enough to go round. I was used to little amounts so it didn't really bother me. To this day I don't eat huge meals and I hate seeing food go to waste. I trace it all back to those days walking in the bush, when we always had enough, but only just enough. I learned just how little it takes to survive. I also know that it could all disappear in a heartbeat. It's good to keep that in perspective, which is why I don't waste things – food, money, friendships or opportunities.

As the sun set on our little camp I don't think I had ever felt so glad to be with my family. They were everything to me. We had no home, no town, no government. All we had were each other, our blankets and the stars above which, since there were no electric lights for miles and miles, shone brighter than I'd ever seen them. It was incredible to be in the bush, falling asleep in the open air, but later I woke in the darkness to the sound of something rustling the leaves nearby and my heart started to race. Militia? Rebels? Soldiers? I pictured them surrounding us, ready to shoot. Just as I was about to wake my mother a big bird flew out of the bush. I let her sleep.

The sun came up and my mother gave us each a cup of water to start the day. That was it. I hoped we'd find some fruit along the way, or maybe some roots to chew on, because otherwise there would be no food until nightfall. We packed up our things and started walking straight across the bush. Sometimes there would be a cattle trail, or a path that people had used, but often we were just tramping through the grass.

Soon we reached the jungle, which was hot and slow going. The sun fell through the trees to dapple the ground, but even then it felt like we were walking through a slick green cave and each of us wore the humidity like a heavy suit. My sweat attracted flies, which bit me, drawing blood, which attracted more flies. It was never-ending battle. There were thick clouds of mosquitoes. I would slap them off my face and neck but as soon as I got rid of one another would appear. It was miserable. We walked in the jungle all day. My flip-flops were useless on the slippery tree roots and the mud, and the sharp grass dug into my skin.

I was starving. Eating only a small stew of leaves and roots at night doesn't satisfy or nourish, especially if you've walked for eight or nine hours. We continued trudging through the jungle, my stomach aching as if it had been turned inside out, when my mother suddenly spotted some fruit hanging from a tree.

'Oh children, look at this,' she said, excited.

She picked some of the fruits and broke them open so we each could have a piece.

'It's called *amurok*.'

It tasted sweet and my body flushed with good feeling as I swallowed it. From then on we saw a lot of this *amurok*.

Years later, during my second week in London, one of my classmates, a Scottish girl with pale skin and red hair, gave me a red apple. I'd never seen a fruit like it before; it was so hard and shiny, like a little rock. I bit into it and the flavour took me right back to the forest. It tasted just like *amurok*.

On the second night we stopped and made camp at another abandoned hut. As usual, we lay down together on the grass mat, with the sheets on top of us. My mother and father were on the outside and the younger ones, including me, lay in the middle. I heard movement out in the forest, birds calling and frogs croaking. It was incredibly noisy. Then I heard a rustling sound and, of course, I thought it was a lion.

'How are we going to sleep?' I asked my mother.

'Listen Alek, these are the noises I used to hear when I was young,' she said.

'And you're still here,' I said. 'Nothing ate you.'

'Thank goodness for that!' she said. 'Just look at it as another new experience that will be fun and make you stronger.'

My father pointed out the constellations as we lay there in the fresh air. I suddenly felt safe with all my brothers and sisters beside me and I thought, really, this is a beautiful life. Somehow my parents had a way of making everything seem good.

My joy was short-lived. I woke in the darkness with raindrops falling on my forehead. Soon it was a deluge and I was soaked. I felt like a frog myself. I fell asleep again, but woke at dawn, cold and wet. It was still raining. I smoothed out my flower print dress and put on my flip-flops. I wiped the water

Mayen, my mother, Ajok, my father, Wek and Athian.

Above: My sister Ajok and her husband Anik at their wedding in Wau in 1982.

Left: My brother Deng and my nephew Lual were born in the same year. This is my mother posing with her grandson, on the left, and her son.

My siblings and I posed for this picture at a portrait studio not long before my father died. (L–R: Deng, me, Adaw, Athieng, Akuol).

My brother Athian on a bridge in Khartoum.

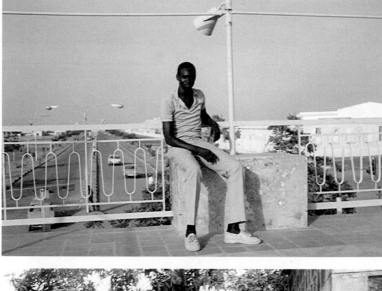

The back yard of our home in Wau.

I was sixteen years old in this photo, wearing my finest denim in this playground near my sister's house.

At my sister's house in London in the early 1990s, with Ajok, her children Awut, Tong and Lual, as well as my brother Deng and sister Athieng.

LI P2028602 3

NAME WEK. ALEK
COURSE ND FDT
CARD EXPIRES 6/6/94

My college ID card from 1994.

Here I am with some of my cousin's wives and my grandparents, as well as Amel, the woman who raised my mother after her own mother died when she was young.

The four women with me are married to one of my uncles.

This child's mother handed her to me and we drove her to the feeding station in El Tonj, where the doctors and others saved her life. I'd seen suffering before, but I'd never seen so many children who were near death from malnutrition. It was overwhelming. That's when I realised what a toll the war had taken on my country.

These women work at the feeding station in El Tonj that is run by Médecins Sans Frontières. Most of them are Dinka women like me.

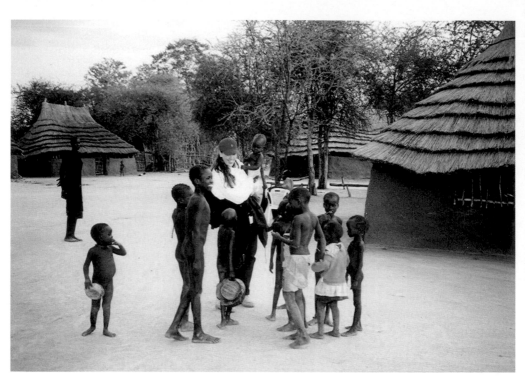

Mora adores children and she had a great time in this Dinka village. The kids hadn't seen many foreigners in quite a while, because of the war, and they kept chanting 'salt, salt, salt' in Arabic. Since there's not much salt in the villages they hoped she'd brought some. Unfortunately, we didn't have any.

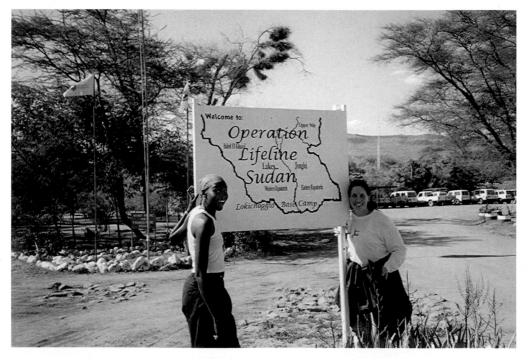

My first agent, Mora, and me near the border of Sudan and Kenya in 2001.

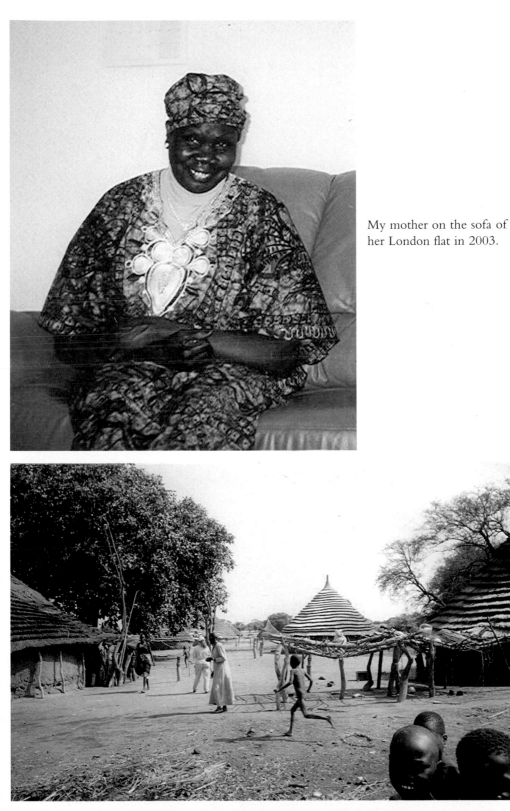

My mother on the sofa of her London flat in 2003.

This is my mother's village, which we visited in 2005.

from my face, brushed my teeth with a stick and started walking with my family, feeling hungry and hoping we'd find some
food. Sometimes I'd just rub my hand on my belly to soothe its
aching. Now, nearly two decades later, the thought makes me
want to cry.

Ever the optimist, my mother found the bright side. She
reminded us that now we didn't need to bathe. She sang silly
songs, made jokes, set up games and told us stories about how
life was when she was young. We'd just been forced from our
home and we didn't know exactly how to get where we were
going, or even if there would be people around when we got
there. Yet here she was in a good mood.

At least there weren't any men with guns. No bombs or
missiles. No planes and helicopters, she said.

We walked like that for two weeks, laughing all day and
sleeping outside in the rain with our rumbling bellies at
night, until one day we noticed cattle grazing and an old man
walking toward us. My father said, 'We're here.' I couldn't
believe it. I felt a big rush of relief that our walk was finally
over. I could see the village where my father's extended
family lived. There were tiny round huts made of mud and
straw, arranged in a line. When I saw those huts I felt a real
pang. Our house in Wau was huge in comparison. I felt sad,
and frightened of how different the village might be from my
home in Wau.

Then people came running toward us and I thought, What
on earth have we got into here? All of a sudden there were
twenty or so kids surrounding us, saying, 'Welcome! Welcome!
Where are you from?' I thought that perhaps it could be nice
after all.

But that didn't last.

'City kids, city kids,' they said. 'We're going to eat you alive!'

They laughed uproariously. I couldn't see what was funny at all.

From that first moment I dreamed about leaving. It couldn't happen soon enough. But I didn't understand war. I didn't realise just how good village life might be compared to that.

CHAPTER 4

We sat under a large tree at the edge of the village and passed a gourd of well water back and forth between us. It tasted so fresh and pure I felt so far from the mud puddles and thirst of our journey. The villagers gathered around us and stared while the elders caught up on the news with my mother and father. My siblings and I stared back silently. Almost all of the villagers were barefoot. Many of the women just had brightly coloured wraps around their waists and no tops. Some of the men wore long beige trousers and tunics but most wore nearly nothing and nearly all of the men carried spears, for hunting or fighting enemies, or scaring the living daylights out of us – who knew? The children, some of whom were completely naked except for a coating of mud and dust, stood leaning on each other, holding hands and looking at us as though we were aliens. I guess that to them we were from another planet, with our rubber flip-flops and our cotton dresses. They weren't used to seeing people who lived in towns. Really, the difference between town life and country life in the Sudan is the difference a century makes. That doesn't mean one is better than the other, but it's impossible not to see a chasm between the two. My parents would have to be the bridge.

I gazed past them and took in the small village in one long look. The shady area where we sat was surrounded by fields of dry stubble from the last millet harvest. Little green shoots of the new crop were just starting to appear. Long-horned cattle stood in a pen nearby, others walked freely through the village. There was a massive round cattle barn with packed-dirt walls and an undulating woven grass roof that rose up to a peak. Behind that a series of much smaller round houses with similar roofs flared out along red dirt paths. You would have to bend low to get through the tiny wooden doorways of the houses. Everything was handmade and worn, stained with sweat and rain. Smoke from cooking fires drifted in low grey rivers that intermingled above the landscape. There was a constant 'bleh, bleh' noise from the lowing cattle. I was relieved to be safe in our ancestral village, and after two weeks of walking with hardly anything to eat I was starving.

One of my father's aunts led us down the path to a group of four little huts and opened the door to our temporary home. Peeking inside I saw a dirt floor, mud walls and a thatched ceiling. Light poured through the gaps where the thatch didn't quite meet the mud wall and the light only illuminated how dirty the place was. This was where all eight of us would sleep. I was grateful, but I was also disappointed. I could see that our lives here weren't going to be easy and I felt guilty for being so spoiled as to worry about that. After all, this was better than what we'd left. I didn't say a word.

That evening we joined our extended family for dinner

around the fire. A group of village children formed a little wall near us and just stood there staring as we sat in the dirt. I salivated at the thought of the hot beef and vegetable stew that we were going to eat, along with *adung*, a hot grain dish. I hadn't smelled meat cooking in weeks, and my stomach was screaming for it. One child, a boy with short hair and bright eyes, wearing nothing more than a pair of pants, couldn't take his big wide eyes off me. When I made a face at him his eyes just got wider. I looked away, but when I looked back he was still staring. Snot dripped out of his nose.

'What do you want?' I said to the boy. 'Why are you looking at me so hard?'

Our hosts, who were my father's cousins, stopped what they were doing and gave me a look. 'A girl does not speak that way,' my father's cousin said. He had fine scars across his forehead, and heavy plugs stretched his ear lobes. He scared me a little.

'But he keeps . . .' I started to say.

'Hush, child.'

My father gave me a look that said, 'Alek, things are different in the villages.' They took the stew off the fire. We squatted in a circle around the pot and when it was my turn I pulled a piece of meat from the stew. What a disappointment. It looked awful, nothing like my mother's cooking. I took a bite and chewed but it made me gag. Looking closely I could see the remains of worms and bugs in the dried beef.

'I can't eat this,' I whispered in my mother's ear. 'It's dirty.'

'I know Alek, but you can't say that. Shut up! We've only just got here.'

I felt ashamed. I didn't realise that in the village children weren't allowed to have their own opinions. Especially about things like food. You eat what you're served.

'Have some, Alek, you're so skinny,' one of the women said.

I really didn't want to eat it but I took another piece of dried beef and forced it down, worms and all.

'You'll never make it being so skinny,' the woman laughed.

I smiled and chewed and hid the fact that I wanted to throw up.

'Eat, eat,' the woman said.

I went to bed on a blanket that night, curled up in my sister's arms. It did feel good to be full, even if there were worms in my belly. I was going to have to learn how to be a village girl, or else I was going to starve.

In the morning I walked out into the bush to use Mother Nature's bathroom. When I came back my mother was pounding grain with a big wooden mortar and a six-foot-tall pestle. She'd lift the heavy pestle up with both hands and bring it down hard on the grains, over and over again.

'What's that?' I asked.

'There's no flour here, you have to make it yourself.'

There would be no tea for breakfast today, I realised. I drank a cup of water and got to work sweeping the hut, using a wisp of straw bound together with woven leaves.

'But mother, we only got here last night,' I said. 'Don't we get a break?'

'This is the village, girl. There are no breaks.'

I was downcast.

'You'll get used to it.'

The work went on. My sister ground more flour for our meal later in the day. I collected the okra someone had given us and spread it out in the sun to dry.

My mother's cows had arrived in the village, delivered by a man from Wau, a member of my father's clan who had known where to find us, so my mother had been up since about four o'clock, milking them straight from the teat into a long-necked gourd. Now she was shaking the cream back and forth, back and forth, to make butter. She cooked that down to clarify it into ghee for cooking, then she started turning some of the milk into cheese and putting the rest of the milk aside to make yogurt. She asked my sister and me to collect the fresh dung and spread it out to dry; we'd burn it in the evening, as the smoke would keep the bugs away.

We worked all morning to get everything organised for dinner, but meanwhile we didn't get a bite to eat. I quickly learned that people in the villages never ate more than once day, unless it was some fruit or nuts they found growing in the bush. Us children would always be out there looking for something to eat. The other children from the village would help us find the right ones, but they never stopped making fun of our accents. Or our looks. Or our clothes. We were a big joke for them.

'Alek, will you go to the well?' said my mother as the afternoon waned.

I walked down the trail towards the well. An old woman stared up at me from her stool as I passed. Her metal necklaces seemed to lift her chin and I thought I saw a glimmer of a smile in her eyes, even though her face remained impassive. There was something very impressive about her.

Down past the cow barn I found the well. If I hadn't been paying attention I would have fallen right in. It was a perfectly round hole, six feet in diameter and lined with ridges that showed how it had been chiselled out of the earth with sticks and shovels. Two wooden planks had been set across the top. Looking down into the darkness I tried to imagine being the man who dug the bottom few feet. There would be no way out.

My mother had given me an empty cooking oil container for carrying the water back to our hut. Back in Wau we'd had a pump and I just had to stick the container under it and move the lever up and down. This well was much more difficult. You had to walk out on the wooden planks and drop the bucket down into the well. It was tied to the planks so the rope wouldn't follow the bucket down to the water. But what was to keep me from falling in when I tried to hoist the bucket back up? Standing at the edge of the pit was so dizzying that I almost turned and walked away, but I couldn't face my mother without water. Then some village kids showed up.

'City girl, don't you fall in.'

'You're a scaredy cat. Nya, nya.'

I flushed with shame.

'What's wrong with your face, girl?' asked one of them.

My psoriasis. I didn't answer.

She was a tall girl, maybe twelve years old.

'You don't know how to do it, do you?' she said.

I shook my head. I was scared of her. Scared of the well.

'Let me help you,' she said kindly.

She smiled and it felt like she was saving my life. The other kids quietened down and together they helped me fill my container. Suddenly I felt a little more at home in the village. I hoisted the water to my head and walked back to our hut with a smile on my face. When I passed the old woman with the necklaces she looked up from her stool and lifted her fingers in greeting.

She was so regal in all her jewellery. The Dinka don't have

much of a history of representational art – traditionally they never painted on canvases or paper, or even on stones or wood. Instead, they would decorate their own bodies with paints, scars and beaded necklaces, shoulder pads, and other items made of ostrich shell, ivory and metal – even Venetian glass beads brought long ago by European traders. The men could be real dandies; some even wore tight beaded corsets at special times. The old woman on her stool was such a rich representation of our culture that she made me feel proud. She'd waved at me! I no longer felt quite such a stranger in the village.

At that time there were over a million Dinka living in the southern Sudan. In the years since so many have fled or been killed that it's hard to say how many are left, but we have always been the largest group in the region. It's believed that ancestors of the present-day Dinka were the first people to bring domesticated cattle from Egypt south of the Sahara desert, where they settled in the flood plain of the White Nile. The Dinka of today probably solidified as a group around AD 1500 and we've fought off invaders ever since, from the Ottoman Turks in the nineteenth century to the invaders of our most recent civil war.

Originally, the Dinka didn't live in villages all the time. Each group, of up to perhaps a hundred families, would follow their cattle from pasture to river, depending on the season. The women and children would sleep inside temporary homes and the men would sleep with the cattle in their mud-roofed pens. These days most villages are permanent settlements, although some members of the clan will still drive the cattle to pasture and to the rivers when necessary.

In the Dinka language we call ourselves the *Moingjaang*, or

'people of the people', and our family ties are vitally important. Just as we counted on my father's distant relatives to help
us escape the war in Wau, any Dinka feels sure that his blood
relatives will do anything within their power to help him when
he's in need.

Clans are traced through the male line – women become
members of their husband's family on marriage. It's said that if
a man doesn't produce a son he will never become an ances-
tor and will therefore be condemned to an eternity of oblivion
when he dies, as there are no heirs to continue his line. To prevent this, if a boy dies before he can marry, his brother or
another relative will take a wife in his name and any children
born from that wife will be considered to be children of the
dead boy. The same is true if a man dies before his wife has
children – his brother will father children with his widow and
they'll be considered the dead man's offspring.

Obviously men dominated the village, or thought they did,
as in most places on earth. Polygamy was common. My father
never had more than one wife, because he and my mother just
didn't think it would work very well, but lots of men, especially in the villages, had two or three. Some tribal leaders have
had several hundred wives, which is a true sign of wealth since
the husband had to hand over a lot of cattle to buy each wife.
The Dinka are careful to avoid marrying within their imme-
diate clan, to avoid inbreeding.

Girls are taught at a young age to cook outside over a fire,
and I was no exception. In the villages the basic foods are
millet porridge, milk, vegetables and spices. Men will fish or
hunt game such as deer and crocodiles, but these aren't part of
our staple diet and, while we ate beef in the village, it was only
when a cow died of natural causes or as a ceremonial sacrifice.

Dinka rarely kill a cow just to eat the meat and it's considered vulgar and unhealthy to eat an animal you find lying dead in the forest or on the side of the road.

In the countryside, the women traditionally plant and tend to the crops, such peanuts, grains, beans and corn, and the men look after the cattle. Cattle are so central to our culture that a man will in a way fall in love with a special cow, giving it a private name and singing songs to it. The Dinka man 'marries' his cow, although the relationship is spiritual and symbolic, rather than 'real'.

One day the elders of the village directed a group of ten- to sixteen-year-old boys from the surrounding area to shave their heads. That night they brought them together to sing traditional songs telling stories of the clan. There must have been fifty boys and men there, some of the men wearing beaded corsets and kilts woven from cows' tails. Most carried spears or long branches with leaves at the end. Several men beat a drum that they had made by burning out the insides of a log.

I could hear them chanting and singing all night. The songs were stories about the village, where the people came from and about Dinka who had done important things. Since they had no pens or paper, the village storytellers preserved their people's history in these songs, passed down through the generations. As the songs went on and the hour grew late the boys fell into a trancelike state, or fell asleep sitting up, and in that way they passed the night.

At dawn their parents led them to a clearing where they sat cross-legged. An elder held a sharp knife to the first boy's skin and then twisted his head so the knife sliced fine, feathery lines into his forehead as the boy called out the names of his ancestors. Blood poured down his face but he did not scream. Crying out would have shown him to be a coward, and it also might have caused the knife to slip, making an uneven scar that would have marked him for life as a weakling. He was a man now, able to herd cattle, hunt and protect the village from invaders. After the scarring ceremony the boys' fathers wrapped large leaves around their heads to cover the wounds.

Looking at these newly minted men, with their blood dripping into the dirt, I felt both sick and proud. My father had the same scars. I turned to look at my mother and for the first time the scars on her arms made sense to me. Then I panicked – what if they wanted to scarify me? The Dinka women of old wore ritual scars. My aunt had told me about squatting in the dirt and being held down while a man sliced her face.

Sure enough, after I had been in the village for a few months, the older women started talking about how it was my time. I freaked out but my mother put her foot down. She and my father wanted their daughters to do well in the modern world, in the cities, without scars to forever mark us as outsiders. So, despite the indignation of the village elders, they refused to let anyone take a knife to my face. Thank goodness for that.

Curiously, in my own family it was my mother, not my father, who was obsessed with the cows and made sure they were cared for. Although he grew up in a village and understood everything about cattle, my father really was a modern man, more accustomed to walking with his briefcase down to the office than grabbing a spear and heading out into the bush. Plus, his bad hip made it hard for him to get around. The villagers must have seen us as an odd family.

My mother's name, Akuol, means 'gourd' in Dinka. It's very appropriate because gourds are incredibly useful and important to life in the villages. We dry them and use them as serving pots, storage pots, everything. When they crack, we'll sew them back together. You can keep using them for a long time.

In the village, my mother was like one of the gourds – very utilitarian. She got things done and her industriousness made her the envy of many people. Even her cows were envied. I remember that some of the other families coveted her best bull, which was tall and broad, a good stud animal. My mother would breed him with her cows and get quite valuable calves. One morning a herder brought his cows past my mother's small herd, pretending to be casual about it. But he lingered for a bit too long. It turned out he wanted to trick my mother's bull into mounting his cow, for free. My mother told him he couldn't use her bull unless he paid for it. The man walked on.

Another morning I was woken by my mother shaking me by the shoulders.

'Alek, get up, my cow is giving birth and she needs help.'

We ran out in front of the hut and there was the cow, moaning and looking like she was going to collapse. Her tongue hung out of her mouth and she seemed so desperate that I started crying.

'Alek, there's no time for that. Come, hold her.'

I put my arms around the cow's neck to stabilise her while my mother went behind.

'That's right Alek, keep her steady.'

I stepped in a pool of warm and sticky blood with my bare feet. My mother was talking to the cow.

'Good girl, good girl.'

69

My mother really loved that cow. She reached into her and gently groped for the calf's hind legs – it was in breech. The cow stared into my eyes with the typical vacant look, but I thought she must be very upset.

'Straighten up,' I ordered her.

She was surprisingly still.

'Here she is!' said my mother.

She pulled. I could see the strain on her face. Then her front legs almost collapsed as the calf came out and fell to the ground. She groaned and inhaled. The calf was alive and healthy, spotted grey and very pretty.

Half an hour later the calf was nuzzling her mother for milk.

'You did a good job, Alek,' my mother said.

Nothing made me happier than her praise.

Dinka people are expected to behave honourably and with dignity. To the outside world our bearing – standing tall, chin up, prideful – might make us seem a little bit arrogant. We don't mean to appear that way; we have an equal need to be kind and respectful, and generous to others, especially to fellow Dinka. All Dinka are expected to offer their time, food and courtesy to each other. When the communities have problems people gather in public meetings where the chief listens to everyone discuss their disputes and then settles them.

Traditionally, each village had a strong leader called the 'spear master', who received his wisdom and power from spirits. The British colonialists worked hard to eradicate this practice because they didn't want such powerful village figures to disrupt their imposition of colonial rule. Nowadays there is less reverence for the tribal leaders, although the spear masters still have influence in many of the rural villages. While the modern world checks in every once in a while, in the form of trucks, bush pilots, who risk their lives delivering people and goods to remote areas of Africa, and the occasional tourist or researcher, the rural Dinka culture has remained very traditional. Our village, which was populated by my father's relatives, had no electricity or running water. I remember some knives and cooking pots but there weren't any radios – or radio signals to pick up – or lights of any kind, other than the moon and stars at night. Even candles and lanterns were rare.

While I'm not that religious, my people do believe in a deity called Nhialac, who created all life. We communicate with him by way of spirits and rituals that we perform when someone dies or is born, or when someone is sick or in crisis. Sometimes cattle are sacrificed as offerings to Yath and Jak, the primary intermediaries between us and Nhialac. Historically, the Dinka have resisted converting to Islam, but the Christian missionaries have been very successful. These days about one in twelve Dinka considers themselves Christian, though most of the Christians, including my mother, still practice many traditional Dinka rituals. Once a Dinka, always a Dinka, really.

Its not like we have a Dinka holy book and a set of rules, with certain things we do each week. Our spirituality is much more fluid, with no real distinction between the supernatural and the natural worlds. The rural Dinka especially have an almost never-ending contact with the spiritual world through their relationships with their cows and the natural environment. Ancestors fill the spirit world and actively influence the day-to-day lives of their descendants. The spirits, which live in trees, objects such as masks and animals, and even people, act as intermediaries to our god. When something great happens, like rain during a dry period, the Dinka will praise the spirit

71

that controls rain. We can praise, but we can't really question God, because in comparison we're just little specks on the planet.

There is also a strong belief that some people inherit the powers of sorcery and witchcraft and can use them to harm others who cross their path. To counter these spells, Dinka will visit diviners who can track down the witch and remove the spell that has been cast.

One hot morning, when I went outside to sweep the yard, the village seemed to be in a heightened state of excitement. Even the birds were making a lot of noise. It turned out that there was going to be a funeral for a very respected elder of the tribe and the men were preparing to sacrifice a cow.

Later that day we gathered near the dead man's family shrine, an elaborate yet primitive mud and straw sculpture about six feet high. Some men brought a huge white cow and tethered it by both horns to a stake in the ground. The poor thing kept pulling its head back to break free, but to no avail. A man poured milk from a gourd onto the tethering stake. The men recited incantations and then one of them went up to the cow and sliced its neck with a fishing spear. Blood pulsed out of its jugular in scarlet bursts and I felt my own body collapsing from shock. I had to hold my mother's elbow for support. Within moments the cow had fallen to its knees. Then its back legs buckled and it tumbled to the ground. There were smiles all around. I didn't understand. Why did they kill the cow? I realised that the other children were right: I really was an alien. There were so many things I didn't understand.

I went back to the hut and told Athieng and my little

brother Deng what I'd seen. They wanted to run over to see the blood, but I stopped them.

While I never thought of my parents as being particularly lenient, village life taught me just how easy I'd had it in Wau. As a child, I always spoke my mind. I'm usually a very relaxed person, but if I'm not happy about something I say so. When I was a child that was doubly true. My parents respected our opinions, so long as we respected their authority, but in the village the adults were surprised that we had opinions, let alone expressed them. They especially didn't want to get lip from a girl. Every man, and that includes the young men, felt he could boss me and any other female around. If you didn't listen they would give you a smack. They didn't beat you badly, but they certainly let you know what they wanted you to do.

The problem was that my parents had raised me differently. My father treated my mother with respect and was never violent towards her. I didn't understand why the men in the village felt they could hit a girl or, even worse, steal her from her family in the middle of the night and marry her, just as long as they made the proper payment of a few head of cattle. But they could. That happened many times. If the girl complained, no one would help her. The wives were chattels.

People like to romanticise life in the African bush. There are many wonderful things about rural Africa, but for women, the villages can be really rough places. It's true all over Africa.

As the rainy season came to an end the nights began to get really hot. One night the hut was a stifling mud prison so we

73

took our bedding outside. The rest of the village had the same idea. In the dim moonlight I could make out the shapes of sleeping people in front of each hut.

'Mother, what about the lions?' I asked.

'Shush,' she said tiredly.

'A lion would snap you in two, Alek. You watch it,' said my older brother.

'He would?'

'Stop scaring your sister. You keep talking like that and it's going to come true – only the lion's going to eat you, not her.'

With that his eyes opened wide and he looked terrified. We lay on our backs in the darkness, listening. A branch snapped and a bird flew out of a tree, wings beating. I could hear movement out in the bush. Or was it the wind?

'Poppa?' I said.

'Don't worry,' said my father. 'A lion wouldn't come near a village. They're too intelligent for that. No lion wants to end up warming some elder's backside.'

I soon fell asleep to the rhythm of my sister's breathing.

I awoke with the most horrendous rustling noise right inside my ear. I slapped my ear with my palm and it just got worse. I sat up and screamed.

There was a bug in my ear. I screamed again, which woke my mother and father. I was squirming around and clawing at my ear to get it out.

'Mummy!' I cried out.

'What is it, Alek? Be quiet, you'll wake the village.'

That's just what happened. A man's voice came from the group of huts across the trail: 'Damn it, girl, be quiet!'

'She's got a bug in her ear,' my sister called back.

'So?'

'It's driving her crazy.'

'Don't back talk me,' he shouted. 'I'm trying to sleep.'

The village men were angry, unreasonable people. Not like my father, who came over to comfort me.

'Hush, darling,' he said.

Some children walked over to laugh and point at me. I was so upset that I started crying.

'Quiet!' the man ordered.

The bug moved in my ear; I screamed.

The man rushed over and raised a switch to hit me.

'Stop!' my father said.

'You don't tell me to stop,' the man replied, and swung at me. Thankfully he missed.

My father was limping, in no shape to fight, but he stood his ground.

The children were laughing. I was screaming and crying so hard.

'Help me,' I cried.

'You'll just have to wait until it crawls out,' the children said. It felt so cruel.

Then the man whipped me, over and over again until my father finally managed to stop him. I jumped up and ran off towards the bush, clutching my ear.

'Elephants are going to stomp on you,' one of the children cried out.

'Watch out for snakes!' said another.

It was pitch black in the bush, except for the glowing eyes of lions I conjured up out of fear. I just kept running. I'd trip and fall over into the dirt and get up and keep running. I was deep into the bush before I stopped and looked around.

Nothing, I was all alone. I wanted to be at home in Wau, with my mother telling a story as I drifted off to sleep.

I realised that, of course, the villagers were right. There was nothing anyone could do. I was making a fuss out of nothing. I stayed out there until just before dawn, the bug making a racket the whole time. When I came back my family was still asleep on the ground. I started the fire and then sat nearby, watching until each of them awoke. No one said anything about my ear, or the fact that I'd spent the night in the bush.

Sometime that afternoon the noise vanished. The relief wasn't nearly as acute as the bother had been. I never did see what kind of bug it was. Every night after that, I slept with one ear on the bedding and my arm over the other. I fell asleep wishing for the concrete walls and tin roof of our home back in Wau.

I know my problems were just those of a child, and that in comparison to all the hardships my parents and the other adults of the village had to contend with my difficulties were minor. The bug, after all, was just a bug and he didn't stay that long. I learned a lot from my parents while we were in the village. Through it all, my parents retained a hopefulness, an optimism that has really helped them through a great deal of pain. I know that many people would have reacted with anger and rebellion, or by drinking and taking drugs, and I'm so fortunate that they didn't. I think our strong Dinka culture played a big part in that but, even more, it was my parents' basic nature and world-view that carried us through. They saw virtue in pain; they didn't ignore suffering or try to cover it up, but neither did they let it take over their lives. We always had the feeling that as long as we had each other – my parents, my brothers and sisters and I –we'd be all right. I think that's true: we gave each other hope. It's really very inspiring to have absolutely nothing yet still have hope that tomorrow will be a good day. That is a great gift that my mother and father gave me.

As the weeks passed in the village this innate optimism was severely tested. My father's hip only got worse as we waited out the war. One morning I went into the hut and found him curled in the fetal position on his blanket, a strange look in his eyes.

'Help me up, child,' he said.

He seemed like another man, distant, frightened and desperate.

I called for my brother and together we lifted our father. He needed to go to the bathroom so we walked him into the bush. Each step was agonising. In the bush, he waved me away, for privacy. I looked away and held back my tears. I couldn't bear his suffering.

Soon it became nearly impossible for him to bend or sit without falling. Walking was a painful and slow experience. It seemed that he was harbouring an infection inside his pinned hip, but he never complained.

There was an old man who lived in a hut on the edge of the village. I'd seen him now and again. He was very tall and often appeared out of nowhere, covered in white dust. His head was shaved but he left a rough tuft of matted hair on the crown of his head; his v-shaped facial scars were black lines under the dust and he wore a necklace of white bone and indigo-coloured beads with a gold clasp. He smoked a long brass pipe with a stone bowl. His dusty face was bony and stern, looking down on us from his great height. Us children called him 'ghost giant'. He rarely said a word, but when he did speak it came out in a smooth, low voice.

He was said to be a healer. One morning, at my mother's urging, I fetched him to come and examine my father. He put his nose to my father's hip and inhaled. The smell of the infection sent his head back sharply. Then he nodded at my mother and said, 'Doctor. He must see a doctor.'

Here we were, far from the nearest hospital, with no transportation and no hope of finding a surgeon. My father needed the kind of medical attention that nobody in the village had ever even imagined, let alone seen. Without it, he would die.

CHAPTER 5

The rainy season's heavy showers had left puddles and swampy areas all around the village. Mosquitoes bred in the still water now that the rains had ended. We'd burn dung so the smoke would drive them away, and I rubbed dung ashes on my skin, but nothing seemed to work. They were more than a nuisance, because they carried malaria and other diseases. No one in the village had mosquito netting. It was horrible at times, with great swarms of mosquitoes that were starving at the end of the day, just like us. We'd eat. Then they'd eat. Night after night, huddled with my family in our hut, I'd battle the mosquitoes. In the morning I'd wake up with welts and bloody smears from where I'd swatted them. We'd burn more dung, and then the daylight would drive them into hiding.

To my father the mosquitoes symbolised his failure – which none of us perceived – to protect his family from the war and to provide them with a good place to live. Whenever anything went wrong he took it all on his shoulders. He wanted so badly for us to have a better life but he had enough troubles on his own without taking on everyone else's. His hip was killing him and he was desperate to leave the village, but we couldn't return home until the fighting stopped.

Since we had no radio we joked that my sister in London probably knew more about the progress of Sudan's civil war than we did. Everything we learned came from the bush telegraph. My mother asked questions of every outsider who came through the village. Usually it would just be someone from a nearby village, who didn't have much more information than us, but once in a while a relief worker or missionary, or a trader, would come through. For months the news was always bad. The battle was still raging in Wau and people were still fleeing to the countryside. It looked like we were going to be in the village for a while, no matter how sick my father got. Rather than fall into despair because the situation was hopeless, my parents began building a hut so we wouldn't have to borrow one any longer. My mother swapped some of her precious salt for the thatch and other materials. We collected sticks for the frame and mixed mud with straw and dung for the walls and, little by little, our new home started to take shape.

Curiously, just as we were getting ready to start thatching the roof, a textiles trader appeared. He was a coarse man, not from a Dinka clan, with leering eyes, rust-coloured hair and a rough manner. But he was respectful to my mother when she approached him for news of our home town: he saw that she was serious. They talked, and he told her that he had recently passed through Wau. The fighting had destroyed nearly everything, he said, but the most of the militias had retreated and the battles were largely over. The government controlled the airport and most of the town.

My mother and my father sat outside our hut and had a long talk. My little sister and I spied on them through a gap in the wall, wanting to know every detail of what was going on, but they spoke too softly for us to hear. My parents had their own particular ways of listening to each other. My father's eyes homed right in on my mother's face as she spoke, concerned yet excited. She in turn held my father's wrist as he talked, listening intently to each word he said.

'I see you looking, Alek,' my mother said when they'd finished talking. She laughed. 'Come on out here, all of you.'

Deng, Athieng and I squatted before our parents, and Mayen, Adaw and Akuol stood behind us.

'Children, we will be leaving the village soon,' our father said.

'We got some news from the red-headed trader,' our mother said. 'He was in Wau, and he says that things are better there now.'

None of us said a word. As children, it wasn't our place to speak now, but we must have looked happy because our parents smiled.

'It's going to be difficult – there's no kidding about that,' said our father.

'But we must go home so your father can fly to Khartoum and get his hip fixed,' our mother said.

'I'll help him,' said Mayen.

'Me too,' said Adaw.

'We'll all pitch in,' said Akuol.

It all sounded so wonderful. As soon as we got home we'd work out a way to get him on a flight to the city and my uncle, the doctor, would get him into the hospital. My mother and us children would follow as soon as we could. We'd stay in the relative safety of Khartoum until the war ended. We'd get an education. We'd eat sweets! Our lives were going to be great. I was so pleased, but I was also worried about my father. He couldn't take more than a few steps without grimacing in pain. It was frightening to see him like this. We couldn't stay in the village and, of course, we couldn't think of leaving him behind.

My mother decided to buy a donkey to carry him back. Yet while the village had plenty of cows and chickens, there wasn't a single donkey anywhere. The villagers just weren't donkey people. My mother walked three hours in the blazing sun to another village she thought might have a donkey for sale. She arrived, only to find that everyone gave her the same answer:

'You want a what? For what?'

It seemed that none of the tribes in the area used donkeys. One man was very sympathetic after my mother explained that my father was barely able to walk and that we had at least two weeks of travel ahead of us. He even ran off to ask some of his friends if they had any ideas, but he returned with his palms outstretched, asking forgiveness.

'The closest donkey is five days' walk that way,' he said, pointing in the opposite direction of Wau.

My mother returned to the village and her husband's downcast face.

A week after the trader left my mother made us a special breakfast of a cup of tea and some boiled millet.

'Today we leave,' my father told us.

We packed everything into our blankets, rolled up our long straw mat and set off. No one made a fuss when we left. We just walked away into the bush.

Within an hour my father was barely able to move so my brothers helped him along. It was clear that our walk back was going to be very, very slow.

It was the same routine going home as it had been to get to the village: we'd gather provisions during the day and sleep in an abandoned hut or clearing at night. It no longer seemed strange, this was our life.

One morning I woke up shivering, even though it was already a hot day and I was sweating. I felt that my body had been invaded with a heavy force that prevented me from rising. All I could do was shiver. I could barely raise my hand to wipe the sweat from my forehead. My family woke up and began collecting our things, but I couldn't move.

'Alek, get up,' my mother insisted.

I rolled over and pushed myself to my knees. Standing was difficult. My head ached and my muscles felt like they were filled with pins.

'Are you OK?' my mother asked.

'Yes.'

I didn't want to drag the family down. We already had enough to worry about. We started walking, but I could barely keep up. All morning I shuffled along, hanging back with Deng and my father, who was always the last in line. The others never went more than about ten minutes ahead. With all the time we'd spent living so closely in the village, and our fears of running into militia or other soldiers, we never wanted to be far from each other. We travelled as a pack. But, between my father and me, we were going awfully slowly.

'Something is wrong with you, child,' he said to me.

'No, I'm fine.' We kept walking. At one point I had to stop and lean over to retch bile.

'Alek? Even I'm walking faster than you.'

'Baba,' I said, using the name I'd called him when I was a toddler, 'I'm so tired.'

'I think you've got malaria,' he replied.

Malaria is endemic in the southern Sudan; each year it kills and sickens thousands of people because so few people can afford the mosquito netting that could prevent it. Malaria is caused by a parasite that lives in the blood. When an Anopheles mosquito bites an infected person the microscopic parasite enters its bloodstream. Then when it bites you the parasites mix with the mosquito's saliva and enter your bloodstream.

The parasites travel around your body in red blood cells until they reach the liver, where they reproduce. After a week or so, though sometimes not for several months, the infected red blood cells burst and the parasites attack other red blood cells. As more and more cells rupture they release toxins that make you feel like you have the worst case of flu imaginable. I just kept walking with my father. There was nothing I could do. My mother had some medicine in a syringe that she could use if the malaria got really bad, but my father didn't think my case warranted it. So I walked on, all the time feeling like I was dying. Now and then I'd throw up near the trail. I felt dreadful, yet close to my father: he and I were the invalids in the back of the line, struggling to get through the day. Finally the sun began to set and we made camp.

'If you still feel sick tomorrow we'll take a break,' my mother said.

That night I slept and shivered. I woke up in a hot sweat and the sky was filled with stars. It was a clear, bright night and I thought, This is unbelievable. I was comforted to see constellations that my mother had pointed out when I was young. The stars always gave me solace.

I fell asleep again and when I woke to the sound of my mother washing up after breakfast I realised that I felt better. She'd saved me some stew from the previous night's supper, so I ate that and then we began to walk. By this time, my flip-flops were more floppy than anything else. The straps had broken and I'd replaced them with twine that cut into my toes. There were holes in the soles. Half the time I carried them and just walked barefoot as my feet had developed thick calluses from wandering the village barefoot. I wanted to save my flip-flops for rocky parts. At times our route would take us through a type of tall, sharp grass that could even pierce through the sole of a flip-flop. When a blade of grass hit one of my psoriasis sores I'd yelp.

'Oh my God, this is crazy,' I said as we crossed a field of this grass.

'Just imagine me as a child,' my mother said. 'We never had any kind of shoe at all. We just walked barefoot through everything. The soles of my feet were like leather.'

I loved when it rained because the water felt cool on my feet, but the storms were rare and brief, since the rainy season was ending. When it rained at night we'd sleep right through it and wake up in wet clothes, knowing that it wouldn't take the morning sun long to dry everything. If it rained during the day we'd twirl and jump in the heavy drops. The water was warm and felt like a bath. We would collect as much rainwater as we could carry. When we stopped for a rest my mother would light a small fire and boil the water to kill any parasites. There weren't any people around to contaminate the puddles we collected the water from, but there were plenty of animals in the area. No matter how thirsty we were we had to wait for the water to boil. That's part of the reason we didn't get very sick. We would drink just a little bit of the boiled water, and then carry the rest in a bottle. Late one night I heard my older sister Adaw crying out for one of her old teachers. It made no sense at all, and when I shook her I realised she was still sleeping. In the morning she didn't get up with the rest of us. She just stayed under her blanket, shivering.

'Malaria,' my mother said.

She had it about twice as bad as I did. We spent the whole day fanning her and putting damp cloths on her forehead. Nothing seemed to help. That night she kept us all awake with her feverish nightmares. Early in the morning, just as the sun sent its orange glow over the horizon, my mother decided to inject my sister with the single ampoule of medicine that she had been carrying. A nurse at the German mission hospital where I had been treated for psoriasis had given it to my mother before everyone fled Wau, and she had been saving it for an emergency.

She sent me to fetch water from a pond that we'd passed the night before. Then she boiled the water and the needle over the fire for ten minutes. My sister lay on her side on the sleeping mat and stretched out her long bare leg, turning her head away as my mother, who'd never injected anyone with anything, jabbed the needle into her leg. She must have hit a nerve or something as my sister suddenly jerked her leg and the needle moved sideways. My mother injected the medicine slowly, but as she withdrew the needle blood spurted out of my sister's leg. We wiped it with a cloth and water.

The drug worked. My sister's fever subsided, along with her

86

other symptoms, but her leg hurt where the needle had entered and as the days passed the wound became grey with infection. At night, pus seeped from the wound onto her sleeping mat. With no doctors for hundreds of miles my sister ended up hobbling at the back of the line. Once we reached Wau we would have to find a way to get both of them to Khartoum. I was ten, and I didn't imagine my father or my sister could die. But the situation was clearly dire.

Six months earlier, we had left nothing, arrived at nothing, and were now leaving that nothing for nothing again. We didn't even know if our house would still be standing. We had nothing to be happy about, yet we were happy together as a family.

Nearly four weeks passed this way. It was the beginning of the dry season and our days were sunnier, with more fruits and edible plants along the trail. In some ways the walk was much easier, but as my father and sister were in such pain it took us twice as long to walk home from the village as it had to get there. My sister could still keep walking all day, albeit slowly, but my father was now at the point where he'd have to stop in the middle of the day to rest. My mother would sit with him and look him right in the eye to see how bad he was feeling. I never heard him complain, not once, but she could always tell. Sometimes she would decide that we'd wait and let him rest for the entire day. We would spend the night where he'd stopped. He really felt like he was letting us down.

On his better days my mother pushed us to move along, in her gentle yet insistent way. There was, however, a fine line between trying to hurry him and my sister, so that we could get them medical treatment as soon as possible, and not wanting them to suffer.

We probably added to the delay by taking a different route home – that's typical of any Dinka, in the country or in the city. A Dinka person always changes his return, especially in a time of trouble. You just never know who has followed you, or who expects you to cross their path. There are plenty of bad people in the world. I still drive around Brooklyn on different streets each day. It's ingrained.

Finally, we reached the grassy area that bordered the Jur River, near our home in Wau. I was so excited that I ran ahead of everyone with Athieng, our feet getting sliced up by the sharp grass, which seemed much dryer and rougher than we remembered. We didn't care. We just wanted to see the water, and the far bank, which, to us, was home.

We charged down the path, which soon led into a tunnel of six-foot-high grasses that would whip against us as we ran, and we were laughing and calling out to each other. Suddenly the path opened wide: there was an expanse of grey dirt, stone, mudflats with long-legged egrets stepping about. The river was dry. The treacherous river we had crossed months before was, now that we were in the dry season, reduced to a series of shallow, slow-moving streams that we'd be able to cross easily. Even my father. It seemed magical.

I turned back to tell my mother and then I saw them: three men in raggedy clothes, carrying Kalashnikovs, staring at us from a little bluff just ten yards away. The leader wore sandals and a pair of amber aviator sunglasses. The others were barefoot. I froze. My sister looked at me, and then she saw the men. She gasped. The men stared at us and we stared at them, all of us unmoving.

'Who are you, little girl?' the leader said.

I didn't answer.

I was terrified. I guessed that they were rebels, but even the rebels would kill Dinka if they needed something. I knew that soldiers raped girls. I knew they stole children. At that moment I hoped that they would hate me because of my ugly psoriasis and so would not want to come anywhere near me.

Then I heard my mother's voice from about thirty yards away.

'Alek, what are you doing up there? Why did you stop? Let's keep moving. We've got to get to Wau before sunset.'

Right then the men started coming down towards us and I felt the life drain out of me. I would have peed in my knickers, except I'd hardly had any water to drink all day. Any words that I had left me; I went completely silent.

My mother and I had always communicated well, even if it was sign language, but suddenly I was blacked out, couldn't talk, couldn't move. She picked up her step until she reached me. Immediately she locked eyes with the rebels. They looked at her like she was an apparition. She looked so fierce. I was grateful she was so tough.

'Oh, I see why you stopped,' she said to me.

She was so cool. Nothing fazed her.

I, on the other hand, was sure we were going to be left to rot in the hot sun.

Then she recognised one of the guys. They were Dinka, from Wau.

'Aren't you Anok Deng? I know your mother.'

The leader nodded. He suddenly seemed sheepish.

'Oh my goodness. If your mother only knew. How is she?'

'My mother is good, madam. She's in Congo.'

'She's safe?'

'I think so, madam.'

'Are you going to rob us?'

'I don't think so, madam.'

My father appeared behind my mother. He smiled at the men. He knew them too.

We ended up giving them all of our goods – our salt, a little bit of soap, a cooking pot and our food – but as a present, not because they demanded it. We hoped that we wouldn't need the stuff once we got home. From the look of these rebels, they needed everything and anything that they could get their hands on. The rebel army was full of young men who came from nothing. It wasn't like the SPLA had a big, rich government supplying them with uniforms and food. The soldiers were lucky if they had guns and ammunition. They had to scrounge for food themselves.

I actually felt sorry for them. The rebels even carried my father and sister across the muddy parts of the river where it was really hard to walk. I've always been grateful to them. They could have been horrible to us; they could have killed us right there, which is what happened to so many other people when they met soldiers – the army, the rebels, the militias – yet these guys took a chance and treated us as fellow human beings. It was a blessing. I'll never forget their faces.

Across the river, we came to the brewery, and my parents' friend. He had stayed there during all the trouble but luckily hadn't suffered too much. He'd given all the beer away, of course, and after that nobody came near the place. It was too far from Wau to be of any use, really. We walked into his house, which had a cement floor, clean drinking water and a big yard and I said to myself, 'We're out of the bush. Finally.' He and his wife served us an incredible meal of *kissra* and stew made from dried fish. I hadn't eaten that in so long. I felt like

I was in heaven. It was getting dark so we spent the night at his house.

The next morning we set out for Wau with great expectations. It was so exciting to think about being home again. I wanted to listen to the radio and find out what had been going on in the world while we were away, but as we reached the outskirts of the city we learned exactly what had been going on, and it wasn't good.

The first group of houses we came to had been burned down. All that was left were concrete block walls and broken windows. A cooking fire burned in the open-aired living room of one house and an old man sat in the dirt, staring blankly at us as we passed. The road was pitted as tank treads had dug deep tracks in the dirt. At one point a group of trees had been split in two by mortars so their tops hung towards the ground. The police station had been wrecked; there was a huge hole in the wall. Wau was now a sad, scary place and I was very puzzled – how could I feel sad to be returning to my home?

'Everything is different now,' my mother said.

We arrived at home to find the front gate was broken. Looking into the courtyard we could see that another family had moved in. I didn't recognise them.

'Kick them out, they have no right,' Adaw said.

It was shocking to think of other people in our house.

'Wait right here, children,' my mother said.

She went into the compound with my father and they politely, yet forcefully, explained that we had come back. I saw the man look downcast. I thought he was going to get angry. My father pulled him to the side and said something in private. They shook hands. There was something so powerful about the way my father dealt with people. He was always polite and quiet, yet he had a strength that people respected. The family left within an hour. Later, my father told me they had a house on the edge of town that had been partially destroyed. They'd figured we were gone for good. They were going to return to their own place now.

Amazingly, my mother's stores of peanuts and grain, and even some seeds to plant, were still there, buried under straw in a huge clay pot.

There were no police in town to speak of, but neither were there many people. Most of our neighbours had left, although a few had straggled back. At night it was scary, with army tanks rolling up and down the streets and frequent gunfights between militias and the army. You couldn't trust either side.

We tried to resume our old lives as best we could. It was difficult, because my father's job at the Department of Education didn't exist any more, and there weren't any state-run schools left. I started going to a Catholic mission school run by nuns. My mother had decided to leave the cows in the village because it was still so dangerous and she wanted us all to go to Khartoum if we could, but she planted corn, vegetables and peanuts in the yard, and greens that grew quite quickly. We were very poor, really, but I didn't feel bad about it. We had one meal a day, usually, which kept us going.

It wasn't a good life, because we were, basically, imprisoned. Aside from going to school I wasn't allowed to leave the house, especially at night. The militias would wrap scarves around their heads and come out into the darkness to rob and kill. You didn't want to cross them. We'd hear gunfire every night.

Every day my mother would get a back-yard account of which of our neighbours – there were not many left – had been killed. I'd always know when someone died. In the

Sudan, death provokes great sadness in people and they express it with a lot of moaning and crying. The women make a trilling sound that's otherworldly.

Even if I had been allowed to go out there was nowhere to go. All of the after-school clubs had long since ceased. There weren't any sports to play. There was nothing to do at all. Wau was filled with refugees from the countryside, strange-looking people from deep in the bush. Even the part of town where the rich people had lived, with their cars and gasoline-powered generators, had been overtaken by refugees. Despite the people, however, Wau felt empty. It was a dark place. The most fun we had in the weeks after we returned was taking the batteries that my father used for his radio and hooking them up to light bulbs we found for sale in the market. Suddenly, we had light. We stayed up later. We sang and talked. It was great fun and we were all really excited about having lights just like the rich people. All my life we'd used candles and kerosene lamps.

All this time, however, my father needed to leave, to go to a hospital, and my mother wanted the rest of us out of Wau so we could go to decent schools. My mother and father talked about it every day.

They were determined to get us to Khartoum. Since they were so determined, I knew we'd do it. Even though we were struggling I knew that if we had a chance, we'd make it. My mother and father always gave me that confidence.

There were no buses or trains and no one had a car. Anyway, going by road was out of the question. There were too many land mines and a lot of bridges had been blown up. Warriors, some of them children, set up roadblocks here and there, and they would shoot you if you didn't give them what they wanted.

We couldn't just walk to Khartoum, either – the Sudan is

the biggest country in Africa. It would have taken us months, passing through dangerous territory.

The only way out was on an aeroplane. The military controlled the airport, which was on the outskirts of town about thirty minutes' walk from my house. If I was at school and heard a plane coming in I'd jump up and run home. We'd rush to the airport, slowed by my sister and father. We would put them on the first available plane, and we would follow as soon as we could.

All the airlines had long since stopped landing in Wau, but there were military planes. Every couple of days a giant C-51 transport plane would arrive with supplies for the army. You could get on the return flights to Khartoum if the soldiers were in the right mood, or if you had a large bribe.

They weren't, and we didn't, but still, every time we heard a C-51 in the sky my mother would gather all of us together, along with a few clothes, and we'd walk out to the airport, hoping to escape. There was tall grass alongside the muddy road and a choking wetness to the air that made me feel even more desperate. At the airport, the soldiers stood around in their fatigues, their berets cocked on their heads, their eyes bloodshot and nervous. We'd stand in the hangar along with hundreds of other people and no one, including the soldiers, seemed to know what was going on. We'd only know that we didn't get on the flight when the plane pulled out onto the runway without us.

I despised the soldiers, but since they were the same men who shot up the town every night we were respectful towards them for our own safety. If you complained they'd get angry and start shifting their guns around in their hands. They liked to see people beg – that made them feel strong.

It was a shock when they finally showed a little grace.

My father's hip was so bad that anyone could see he desperately needed help. My sister's infected leg was turning black. She couldn't sleep well and walking was incredibly painful. There was no one in Wau who could treat them.

On our third trip to the airport my mother begged the guards to put my father on a flight. She pointed to his hip. She called my sister Adaw over and showed them her leg was poisoned. She really begged. Finally, the guards said, 'Fine, they can go. The rest of you will stay.'

When they flew off there were five of us children left. My older sister Ajok had married a Dinka man and gone to London, where he was studying architecture. They had wanted to return with their children but my parents told them that war was too severe and that the future of the family depended on them staying in England, where they could earn money to help us out or apply to get us refugee status if possible. My oldest brother was studying in Juba. My mother had told him never to return to Wau. Ever. We were going to leave ourselves. There was nothing left for us. We had no father. We had no money. We had no idea what the future held. We went home and wept. It was one of the few times I'd seen my mother cry.

A few days later I heard another plane and we returned to the airport but they wouldn't let us on. And the next time. We were turned away again and again because there weren't enough seats. We were still the Wek Army – there was no way we were all going to get on a flight. Finally, one day, while we were walking to the airport I turned to my mother and said, 'I'm leaving today, no matter what. Even if we have to split up.'

For a moment my mother looked at me as if I was mad, but I could tell she believed me. Something told her to trust me.

At the airport it was the same old scene. Nasty soldiers. Hundreds of people wanting to get out. A line of people who, for whatever reasons – bribes? Connections? – were being allowed to board the plane. This afternoon, like all the others, it looked like we wouldn't get on. I wished we had money for a bribe. As we struggled to persuade the soldiers I spotted one of our neighbours getting ready to board the plane. I didn't know him at all well. He could have been a child molester for all I knew.

I made a decision. Without saying a word I left my mother's side and walked over to him. He was nearly a stranger, yet I told the guards he was my father. Amazingly, he nodded in agreement. I was going to get out!

My mother looked at me with great pain in her eyes, but she understood. In that moment she confirmed her faith in me. I felt scared but very, very strong. I was going to help my father. With me gone, it would be easier for the others to get on the plane. One less Wek in the army.

My mother couldn't talk, for fear of revealing to the soldiers that I was an impostor, so she kept silent. But her face said everything: 'I love you, I'm proud of you. Be safe.'

As the line began to move she whispered to my new 'father' in Dinka:

'Take her to my family in Khartoum,' she said, giving him my aunt's address. She didn't know the address of my uncle's house, where my father was staying.

The man nodded. But who knew? What if he sold me? What if he took me as a one of his wives? What if I never saw my mother again?

As the line began to move towards the plane I glanced over at my mother and smiled. I suppose my face gave it away, because a soldier suddenly stepped in front of me.

'Who are you?' he demanded. 'What are you doing here?'

I acted offended. I acted as tough I could.

'That's my dad,' I said, pointing to my neighbour.

My neighbour kept his cool and just nodded his head.

'Come along, girl,' he said. 'Keep with me.'

I was alone in the world, fleeing a war with nothing more than the clothes on my back. As we headed to the plane I turned to see my mother again. Her eyes were puddles of sadness. I wanted to cry too, but I didn't.

We climbed the metal steps into the cargo hold. The massive old plane was used for hauling supplies to military bases around the country and it didn't have any amenities. But it had propellers, and all I needed was to be lifted over the vast desert to where my father waited in Khartoum. I took a seat next to my 'father' on a wooden plank, and figured out how to strap myself in. There was a parachute underneath the plank, but I doubt it would have stayed on a skinny kid like me if I'd had to use it. As soon as the plane started taxiing down the runway the pilot turned all the lights off, so we wouldn't be shot down by surface-to-air missiles. We flew in total darkness for three hours. The other passengers were completely silent; I felt like we were on a death watch. Finally we landed in Khartoum.

CHAPTER 6

My pretend father led me down the steps to the tarmac, where the heat hit me like a wall. In the airport the man's wife and three children looked shocked when they saw us walking up together.

'And this girl . . . ?' his wife said.

'Don't worry about her.'

The children glared at me.

'Don't you remember Alek? She lived down the street from us in Wau?'

Then they relaxed.

Walking through the airport, I was dazzled – by all the upholstered furniture, the lights and the people wearing nice clothes. It felt really good to be here.

We drove on a crowded road a few miles into the city, where they left me at my aunt's house.

'Alek – I can't believe it,' she said when she opened the door. Nobody had any idea I was coming.

She lived with her husband and their two children in a two-storey house with painted walls and lots of furniture. They even had a television, which I'd seen only a couple of times in my life. Since it was late she told me to spend the night with her. I hardly slept, because I was so lonely for my mother and so excited to see my father.

In the morning my brother Wek came to collect me. I hadn't seen Wek in a long time. He was taller than I remembered, but I felt right at home with him. In daylight my aunt's neighbourhood looked dry and dirty, with unpaved streets lined with brick houses. I almost got soaked by a bucket of water that a woman threw out on the street after washing her dishes.

We caught a bus along a road that was jam-packed with carts and people and cars and buses, to a terminal in the centre of the city. Everything in Khartoum was huge. The buildings were all two and three floors high, with metal gates painted turquoise and blue and curtained windows. I didn't remember ever seeing so many people in one place. Most of the men were wearing long white djellaba and sandals, and the women were in topes, a three-metre length of wide fabric – either brightly coloured or just plain white – which they wrap around their torso and up over their head.

We waited at the terminal in the tremendous heat, my eyes taking in everything. A rich aroma filled my nose and I turned to see that a man had spread a striped blanket on the concrete and was laying out baskets of freshly baked bread on it. Nearby, a vendor sold watermelon slices drizzled with lime juice. A man wearing a brown suit over a T-shirt, with fat red and white beads against his dark neck, stood puffing on a three-foot-long pipe, the smoke obscuring his creased face.

'Would you like a Coca-Cola?' my brother asked me.

'Sure,' I said, trying to be cool about it. I'd seen the Coca-Cola signs around since I was a child, but I had never tasted it. He bought two bottles and handed me one. It was ice cold and felt so good on my hand in the heat. The bubbles tickled my lips as I raised it for a sip. It tasted so rich! But the bubbles – how could I swallow the bubbles? I gagged and the Coke came out of my nose.

'The same thing happened to me my first time,' my brother said.

I drank the rest of the bottle very carefully.

A beaten-up brightly coloured bus pulled in and we forced our way through the crowd that was clambering to get on and found seats. We sat on the bus for half an hour, past block after block of dirty whitewashed buildings with the occasional palm tree or high shrub rising up above the walls.

'Just to warn you – Daddy's not well,' my brother said.

My heart sank. I had pictured my father as cured, walking tall and able to lift me high above his head.

We got off the bus and walked along a dirt street to the house of our uncle. My brother banged loudly on the metal gate before we opened it. There in the courtyard was my uncle's wife. Or rather one of them – he had three. She led me inside to see my father, who was lying on a camp bed in the living room.

'My darling,' he said, sitting up to give me a hug.

I was upset by seeing him in such bad condition but he was glad to see me and my uncle was taking good care of him. Since he had three wives and a dozen children, the three-room house was overrun with people but there was a good atmosphere. It's common in the Sudan for men to have several wives, and my uncle's wives, at least, had worked out a good accord. One of them did most of the cooking. Another took care of the house. The third managed the provisions.

My uncle was a doctor and he had tried to use his connections to get my father treated by a good surgeon, but nothing had come of it. Everyone wanted more money than we had to perform the necessary operations so my father languished. However, my sister's infected leg was treated successfully. My uncle arranged for me to see a few dermatologists about my psoriasis, which just seemed to get worse and worse. None of them had any new ideas. Just the same old creams that the German doctors had given me, which were expensive and didn't have any long-term effects. So with my father sick and no new doctors to see, I spent most of my time just sitting around the house. I felt safe there. I never worried about guns and soldiers.

I missed my mother and my brothers and sisters terribly. Every once in a while we'd get a message from my mother: things are rough; we're still trying to get on a flight out of here. Do not under any circumstances return.

Whenever I could, I'd tag along with my brother or another adult when they went out into the city to run errands. The city itself had about a million people, but when you added in Bahri, where we eventually moved, and Omdurman, which were reached by bridges across the White and Blue Niles, the metropolitan area had about four million people. Refugees had poured in from Ethiopia, Chad and elsewhere in Africa during the 1970s and 1980s and then, when our own civil war started up again, people from all the tribes of the south flocked to Khartoum. It was definitely an Arabic city, with a Sunni Muslim government, but also a cosmopolitan place with many different types of people.

Still, even as a ten-year-old girl I could feel that the Arabic Muslims in Khartoum looked down on me, a little Dinka girl. I spoke Arabic with a heavy accent, since Dinka was my first language and what we spoke at home. All my schooling had been in Arabic, which was mandated by the state, so I could communicate well even though the words I used marked me as a real country girl. I couldn't help but notice the stares as I walked down the street.

The most beautiful buildings in the city were mosques, with their minarets rising above the other buildings. There was a small mosque near my uncle's house that I loved. It was a squat building, painted mint green with small white triangles along the roofline. A fat brown ice cream cone minaret rose up from the roof, wrapped with a band of white that, to me, looked like sugar.

Five times a day the muezzins would climb to the top of the minarets and in a wavering, pleading voice call the faithful to *fard salah*, or mandatory prayer, with the Adhan, in Arabic:

Allah is great, Allah is great
I bear witness that there is no God but Allah
I bear witness that Muhammad is Allah's Messenger
Hasten to the prayer, hasten to the prayer
Hasten to real success, hasten to real success
Allah is great, Allah is great

The men would race to the mosque for prayers, or drop to prayer rugs right on the pavement or in the market. It was quite beautiful to see this level of devotion to God. I remember one somnolent afternoon my brother and I came across a gathering of Muslim Sufi mystics dancing and praying in a square in the old part of Khartoum. One of them, a man in brightly coloured rags, broke from the others and started spinning, pieces of his torn clothes flowing like streamers as he twirled round and round.

There were other aspects of the Muslim world that I couldn't abide. For instance, shariah often seemed outrageous. There was a sixteen-year-old boy who regularly sat on a street corner near my aunt's house. His left arm and his right leg ended in useless stumps. He'd wave them about and demand coins, though I never saw anyone give him any. My aunt told me that he had been caught robbing a small shop and, in accordance with the current interpretation of shariah, he'd been punished by having his opposite hand and foot amputated.

The country was steadily becoming Islamicised. The National Islamic Front had started making children learn radical chants at school; the morals police began to insist that women wear veils. Young couples couldn't walk down the street holding hands. A girl wearing a skirt would be called a whore by strangers. People were arrested and then tortured by prison warders who had been trained by the Iranian Revolutionary Guard. Where once Sudan had been a tolerant place, with peaceful Sufism as the main form of Islam, it had become a harsh place where young thieves were mutilated. In a way, I hated the city, but living there was better than getting shot at in Wau or having a bug crawl into my ear in the village.

After three months the rest of my family arrived. My uncle, Deng, who was not technically my uncle, but rather some sort of second cousin who we just called uncle, was very generous to us.

'Hey, do you mind if my wife and six of my children join us in your little three-room house?' my father had said to him.

It was stressful. Uncle Deng and his three wives and their twelve children slept in the two bedrooms. The Wek Army got the living room, which was fine for us, considering that we had nowhere else to go. We put thin mattresses on the floor and all slept together there. One person would crowd up to the next person and that person wouldn't like the way the person on the other side moved around or talked in her sleep and there would be a lot of complaining because there was only a limited amount of room. Somehow we figured it out every night.

The men and women always ate their meals separately in my uncle's house. Of course the men got more food. I wasn't used to this, because my family had always eaten together, and at first it bothered me. After a while I started to like it. When just the women are gathered around you can talk about girl stuff that you know the men wouldn't want to hear.

No matter how hard we tried to help out with the cooking and the cleaning, it always came down to the fact that we were about twenty people in a three-room house, with two verandas and only one latrine. I'm amazed that they invited us to stay at all. It's a real testament to my uncle's kindness, and to Dinka generosity in general. In the end, however, it was too much for my uncle's family to take. His wives started bickering with each other, which I hadn't seen when my family first arrived. One of the wives was from another tribe, and the other two would berate her constantly for not being Dinka, and not doing things the Dinka way. My mother just said to us: 'Mind your own business.'

We knew we had to get out of there quickly. Neither of my

parents had jobs, but my sister in England was working as an au pair. She started sending us a hundred pounds or so each month. Since there was no mail, and we couldn't trust the banks to give us any money she wired, she'd send a letter with cash via a courier service used by one of the luxury hotels in Khartoum. We had a friend there who we could trust to give us the money. It was like a James Bond film. We'd take the bus to the hotel, where we would meet him clandestinely and he'd hand over the cash.

Once we had money my brother went out every day to find a house that we could afford, which was tricky because Khartoum was much more expensive than Wau. We knew that if he didn't find a place, we'd end up in the refugee camps on the far edge of the city, and living in those tents is no joke. I went out there once with my mother, to visit some of her distant relatives who'd settled in the camp. We walked into the Sahara for half an hour or so until we reached a vast wasteland where the government had settled the penniless refugees. Nothing grew there. Water was scarce. There were no toilets. Some of the people had tents, but most lived in shacks they had put together from sticks, plastic sheeting and cloth. Her relatives were doing relatively well: they had a compound of tents and were searching for a way out. But people kept coming. The camp just got bigger.

When we left in the late afternoon the sky was clear. Within a few minutes a massive windstorm blew up.

'Oh my God, the haboob,' said my mother.

The haboobs are powerful windstorms that sweep up vast amounts of red dirt and black out the sun. They can come any time of the year, but there are more of them in winter. This one was quickly bearing down on us.

'Quick, Alek, behind that rock.'

We ran to a boulder and crouched underneath an overhang. The haboob arrived with a screeching sound. I couldn't see my hands in front of me. The dust filled my eyes and ears. The grit hurt my teeth. We crouched for an hour until the storm passed, and then we walked home, red with dust. We looked like we were wearing make-up. When we got home there was dust in the water; dust in the beds. Red dust everywhere. I thought about the refugees in their flimsy tents and worried that we would end up there.

My brother found us a two-room house on the edge of town.

The new house was walled off from the street. It had an intermittent electricity supply, from which we could power lights and the radio. Since we had almost no possessions moving in wasn't difficult. We bought a charcoal stove, some cooking pots and a ceramic jug to keep the drinking water cool on the 100-degree-plus days.

There were two large rooms for sleeping, one for the girls and one for the boys. We had cotton mattresses, which were a real treat. I'd never slept on a bed like that before – in Wau we'd always used beds with plaited string platforms for mattresses. My sister sent us beautiful sheets from London, so we felt like we were living in luxury even though our floors were made of hard-packed dirt.

We had a latrine with a pit, and we had running water, which was a first for me. Curiously, there was no drain for the water. Instead, there was a holding tank. When you took a shower the run-off would go into the tank, which held about three showers' worth. When the tank was full we'd scoop the water out and spread it out thinly over the street. For some reason the Khartoum soil didn't absorb water well so if you just dumped the water it would puddle up and take for ever to drain. We spread it out thinly on the street so it would evaporate quickly in the sun. There were people down the street who didn't bother to do this and there would often be a disgusting puddle of soapy, scummy water in front of their house. My mother couldn't stand the way they lived.

One day we were walking home when a car drove through the muck and splashed it up on us.

'I've got to go back to Wau,' my mother said.

She was such a stickler for order. In her house, children did chores. We swept; we washed; we cleaned the yard; we filled up the bucket, washed our laundry by hand and hung it to dry. Every weekend it was work, work, work. But we always had clean clothes. To her, disorder was a sign of laziness.

'How do you feel about yourself if you're messy like that?' she'd say.

Khartoum is such a hot place we'd often take the beds outside to sleep. From the back yard we could look into the neighbour's house, which was like a palace. It had big windows, and we could see their beautiful tiled floors, which were covered in intricate rugs. The sound of the television would come out of their rooms. They ran their air conditioning on hot nights. I'd never been so close to such wealth. Not that I got to know them – they never spoke to us. I'd lie on my bed outside in the sweltering night listening to their air conditioning and looking up at the stars while sweat dripped off my chin. Khartoum would get so hot that plants couldn't live, except along the riverbanks where there's always a wide green strip of grass and shade trees. The river was far from our home. Once, we tested the heat by cracking an egg on a stone on the terrace – it fried right away. We ate it, too. Khartoum is an uncomfortable place and we had to struggle to make our lives decent.

Even though we were far from the war we always lived in fear of death. One morning I woke up shivering. My mother tried to get some hot tea down me, and some bread, but I refused. Then I started vomiting. I kept that up until bile came out. It was malaria again. I have no way of knowing if it was a new bout or a recurrence of the old, but it happened several times. There were diseases all around. Our neighbours got typhoid. Someone across the road died of diphtheria. None of us were vaccinated against anything. Death was a reality we saw daily. It was always around the corner.

My father, for one, was dying, although none of us could admit it. He'd had a stroke. He'd fallen. He was paralysed on his left side and, in addition to his broken hip, he had broken his left shoulder. He just got weaker and weaker until he stayed in his room day and night because moving was too painful. We didn't have the money to get him treated in Khartoum. Though he never said it, he was miserable. We all spent a lot of time trying to cheer him up.

We got the idea to improve his life by improvising a carpet in his room, which was also where the boys slept. The dirt floors were just too awful. You couldn't help but get it on your clothes and feet while walking around. Sleeping could be a dusty nightmare. One day my mother found a freshly dug well not too far away. The workers had shovelled sandy soil out in search of water and left the clean sand in a pile. My mother sent her Wek Army over there with every container we had to bring back sand. We spread it across the floor to make a clean carpet. That little idea of my mother's improved our lives immensely. After that I loved sitting on the sandy floor talking to my father. Despite his illness we all felt safe from war.

I always feel for the poor, because I know what it's like to be poor. It's not fun. The life is forced on you. You feel you have no way out. You don't always have food. You can't buy clothes. You don't go out. The worst part is that you can't afford to be unhealthy. You can't see doctors. You know you're sick, and that you're going to die, but there's nothing you can do about it. That's what happened to my father. My father died from poverty.

It broke my heart to hear my mother and father talking in the dark about what they could do – or couldn't do – to help him get better. My sister wanted him to come to England for treatment but he couldn't get a visa. He would have lived if he'd gone there, but they needed proof that, as an adult, he could care for himself. He couldn't. I remember praying for someone to help us out, but Khartoum had millions of people who needed help. We were just one family in a vast field.

It was awful to see him suffering. I'd go to his bedside and talk to him about my day at school, about the food we were cooking. I'd hold a cool cloth to his head and wipe his lips. His eyes were still bright, even to the end, and he would look at me with such love. He never complained, not once. I remember him smiling at me. He died, in bed, at about fifty-six years old. Athian Wek, my father. My mother was at his side when he passed. Children weren't allowed to see the body or attend the funeral but, curious as I am, I sneaked into the room and saw him lying there, peacefully, and my mother sitting by him. Then they whisked me away to another house. My mother wore white for forty days, because that's what a Dinka woman does when her husband dies. Then she gets on with her life. That's something I learned from my mother: remember, but move on.

After my father died we stayed in the house in Khartoum. Our kitchen was a typically ramshackle affair at the back of the house, with some plates and about five pans. Since there was no refrigerator we had a large clay container that we could put food into to keep it relatively cool. We also had a clay water jug in the corner, with a tin cup always resting on a plate nearby. I'd be super-hot and would walk in that dark kitchen where it was such a pleasure to dip the cup into the water and take a long cool drink.

All the girls helped with the meals. We cooked *kissra*, aubergine and peanut butter, and grilled meats over a charcoal brazier, and washed the dishes in a tub. There was a table where we could sit and eat. Everyone in that neighbourhood grew food, like okra, rocket and tomatoes, because nobody had much money to spend. When we shopped it was only at the open-air market, where different vendors would set up tables with meat and produce. There were little stores around the neighbourhood that sold cold drinks and the like, but we could rarely afford them.

One of my favourite meals was peanut butter salad. I'd chop up some tomatoes and onions and mix them with rocket to make a really dense salad, and maybe add some chopped green peppers. Then I'd mix salt and vegetable oil, along with freshly squeezed lime juice, and stir in a few spoonfuls of freshly ground peanut butter. I'd slice a baguette in half and fill it with salad. That would make a delicious dinner – especially with a few shakes of hot sauce.

We didn't eat breakfast and I usually ate bean stew at school, but we'd always eat the evening meal together as a family, which I really enjoyed. We'd have okra and dried beef stew, or lentil soup, or, if we were really lucky, chicken, or rice, which was even more expensive than flour. We'd have great conversations out there in the yard, laughing and carrying on. The yard was pretty stark, with the bare dirt and cement block walls, so we collected used oil containers, painted them bright colours and planted lovely red, white and purple flowers. We had to water them at least once a day to keep them from dying in the Khartoum heat.

My mother was very strict about whom we saw and where we went. Often, in the afternoons, we'd go to a friend's house and watch an Egyptian comedy show on television. But Khartoum only had television broadcasts from about five in the afternoon until nine at night, so our options were pretty limited. On Fridays, the Muslim day of rest and worship, the television showed nothing but prayers in Arabic. Sometimes I'd pass the time doing school work, or reading a magazine, but the one thing we used to do that I really loved was getting together with my sisters in the yard to make up new lyrics to the songs we learned in school. Or we'd play dodgeball. But mainly life in Khartoum was very dull.

I had one close girlfriend, an Arab girl who lived nearby. My mother didn't mind if I went to her house so we'd spend a lot of time together. She used to teach me how to write Arabic better and we became part of each other's families. Her mother always gave us nice drinks. I liked spending time at their home. Then, one day, I knocked on their door and her mother answered.

'Can I see her?' I asked.

'She can't come,' her mother said. She looked really nervous.

'Why not?'

'She's sick.'

Something in her mother's face made me frightened for my friend. I could tell something was wrong. I wanted to see her but I didn't want to be disrespectful. Still, I thought, she'd been so healthy the day before.

'What happened?' I asked.

Her mother didn't reply. I felt really scared.

'I want to see her.'

Her mother shook her head.

'Please, only for a moment?'

Her mother turned her head as if to say, 'Go ahead, but don't pretend that I let you.'

I ran past her and found my friend lying in bed with a terrified look on her face. She wouldn't say a word to me. There were bloodstains on her sheets.

'What happened?' I said.

She just looked at me with a blank expression, tears in the corners of her eyes. Then her mother came in and she turned her head to face the wall. I looked up at her mother, unable to figure out what was going on. Her mother shooed me out of the house. I stood outside in the street for a while, hoping for some kind of answer.

At home I asked my mother what was wrong with her.

'Those people can do awful things to their girls,' she said.

I asked her to explain but she didn't want to talk about it. I couldn't get it out of my mind.

The next day I went back to see my friend and her mother said she wasn't well enough for visitors. I went back home and pleaded with my mother to explain what happened. I told her about the bloody sheets. She looked furious, not at me, but at my friend's family.

She told me that some of the Muslim families have a tradition of circumcising their daughters when they turn thirteen. They took a knife and cut out the girl's genitals – her labia and clitoris – and then they sew the vagina shut with a needle and thread. I could barely understand what she was talking about because I knew so little about women's bodies. When my mother said that circumcision left only a tiny opening for the pee to come out I felt faint. And when she said that the women had to be cut open again when they had babies I felt furious.

'I want to kill her family,' I said.

'I know what you mean,' my mother said.

She told me that the girls don't get painkillers before being circumcised, and that often they die afterwards from infections. It's all part of 'becoming a woman'.

How could they do that? Imagine growing up like that. Going through puberty. It's horrible. They cut you up and throw away pieces of your body.

'Who does it?' I asked my mother.

'Often, a woman,' she said. 'A woman comes and does it with a razor blade. But the men insist on it too. A man like that would never marry a girl who wasn't circumcised.'

'Do Dinka do this?'

'Don't worry. No one will ever do that to you. It's not the Dinka way.'

My friend healed, and we remained close. She never talked about what had been done to her but after that I couldn't look at her mother or her father. I never wanted to play in their house again. There's a reason God gave women everything they have. To this day women all over Africa are circumcised. It makes it hard for them to go to the bathroom, to menstruate, to have children. They risk infections and countless other problems. It messes up their minds. Just learning about it messed up mine. I became quite rebellious after that.

My older brother, Mayen, who was eight years older than me, used to boss me around. Like most Sudanese men he felt that he could order any woman about. One day, not long after my friend was mutilated, he told me to get in the kitchen and clean the dishes. I said I'd had enough and told him off using curse words, which were forbidden in our house. He was shocked and angry, but instead of telling me not to curse he pulled off his belt. I was afraid he was going to start beating me with it. There was no way I was going to take that, so I ran. I ran out of our yard and into the street, where I sat on a wall and cried, furious. I stayed outside for hours, until it got so dark that I got frightened. When I went inside everyone was asleep except my mother, who had waited up for me. She gave me something to eat and held my hand as I fell asleep.

We got money from my sister in London each month and my father got ten pounds a month in government pension, but that stopped when he died. My mother had to hustle. Since Khartoum was under shariah law liquor was absolutely forbidden and the penalties against it were stiff. But, of course, people still liked to get drunk, as they do everywhere in the world. My mother saw an opportunity.

She rigged up a simple still like the one she'd used in Wau. It produced about one small bottle a day from different grains. One of my aunts offered to sell it to people she knew. When it came to the time to deliver the bottles to my aunt, we were all frightened that my mother would get arrested by the morals police and thrown in jail. We couldn't risk losing her. I volunteered to take it across town.

'They'll never suspect a girl of smuggling liquor,' I said.

My mother agreed. We poured the liquor into small bottles and wrapped them in paper so they wouldn't clank. Then I put them in the bottom of a bag with a cloth on top, so it looked like I'd just come from the market. I was sweating with nervousness as I left the house with one of my brothers. Carrying the bag, I walked towards the bus stop. There at the corner was a policeman. I almost turned around and ran back home, but I forged ahead. As I passed the policeman he stared at me. I lowered my head submissively and looked at the ground. He didn't say a word.

After a while, I started to feel pretty powerful, knowing I was doing something so forbidden. People who drank were lashed in public with leather whips.

We reached my aunt's house without incident.

'Such a young girl to be doing a man's job,' she said.

When I returned home my mother looked sick with worry.

'You'll never do that again,' she said. 'And I won't be making it any more, either. We have to find another way to make money.'

I had been infected with the entrepreneurial bug so I looked around for other ways to turn a profit. My friends and I were always scraping pennies together to buy roasted pumpkin seeds, called *pasali*, from street vendors. I realised that there was no reason to throw my money away on the seeds. Why not just roast them myself, sell some, and eat the rest?

I bought raw seeds, prepared them and then sold them in

little paper sacks at school. I was surprised at how easy it was to make money. Every day I'd bring the money home and give it to my mother. She thought this was a much more sensible way to bring in extra cash.

My psoriasis continued to ravage my skin. Every day my mother would take a sharp knife and cut off the flaking bits because I shed my skin like a snake. My head was particularly bad. She shaved it and coated it with Vaseline and medicine. Nothing helped. My palms were so cracked they bled. That was difficult, especially at school.

I went to a school for immigrants at the edge of town, about forty-five minutes' walk from my house, in an area where people lived in shacks made of cardboard and corrugated metal. It was a poor school, haphazardly put together, though it was better than the school one of my sisters attended. There, you had to carry your own folding chair back and forth to school so that no one would steal it during the night. At least at my school we had benches that stayed in the classrooms. But that neighbourhood was much worse than where we lived. I felt rich each afternoon when I arrived back at our house, having walked by the shacks filled with people whose faces were marked by desperate looks.

My school taught in Arabic, with an emphasis on Muslim teachings. They punished us with canes. If I was late to school, or I did anything wrong, the teacher would ask me to stand erect and hold my palms out so he could whip them with a stick. This happened fairly often. Of course, the whip would make mincemeat of my psoriasis and I'd return home with bleeding palms. It was so bad that one of my tendons was damaged enough to ruin the forefinger of my right hand. I haven't been able to straighten it since, because the tissues healed so awkwardly.

My mother worried herself sick about me. Although we were all planning to go to London when we could, she decided that I should be the first, so that I could get treatment for my psoriasis. Since I was a child it was relatively easy for my sister to get me a refugee visa. I didn't have the same problems my father had. I was excited about seeing my sister. It was like a dream – going to London! But first I had to get my passport. And to do that I had to figure out when I had been born.

CHAPTER 7

I don't know my real birthday, other than that it was during the rainy season. My people don't usually keep track of birthdays. But, about thirteen years after my mother gave birth to me in Wau, I needed an ID card and a passport to go to England. For that, she and I had to choose a date. We decided on 16 April, but for no particular reason other than it was in the rainy season. A street photographer took my picture, which my brother Wek took to the police office in the Khartoum business district to get my ID card. They never saw me in person and, looking at the photo of a tall skinny kid with short hair, assumed that I was a boy. My formal ID card listed me as male with an invented birth date. My world has always been a bit unpredictable. Fortunately, my brother was able to change the ID card, and eventually I got my passport.

With the passports in hand my sister Athieng and I applied for the refugee papers that would allow us to leave Africa and fly to London to stay with our sister Ajok. I hadn't seen her since I was a youngster. The plan was that we'd go to school near Ajok's flat in Hackney, East London. I would also help with her children and eventually I'd learn English, get a job and help my sister save money to bring over the rest of our family.

There was little for me to stay for. The economy – after decades of war – was in ruins. My father was dead. It wasn't hard to pack for the trip because Athieng and I owned next to nothing. I had a dress, flip-flops and underwear, and that was about it. Anything else I'd gathered over the years I left for my brothers and sisters. I was going to the land of riches. They wanted to share what I left behind.

'Leave it, Alek, leave it – you're going to get everything you want when you get to London, while we'll be stuck here,' one of my older sisters said as I was packing my stuff to leave. She wanted a little metal hair clip I'd had for years.

'Get yourself a coat quick when you get there. London will be freezing,' said Adaw.

My last night with my family was sweet, but sad because I was so attached to my mother. We talked and Athieng and I sang some silly songs. We had a good last meal of *kissra* dipped in stew. I was going to miss them all terribly. After dinner my mother told me to have a shower. She believed in good grooming. It didn't matter if I were going to visit neighbours or travelling halfway around the world. She wanted me to look good in order to represent the family well. I dressed in a purple shirt and skirt that my mother had purchased for the occasion.

Properly attired, I joined my siblings and my mother in a neighbour's car and set out for the airport in the desert night, the stars above lighting the streets of Khartoum. The city had no streetlights to speak of back then, and hardly anyone was

119

about at night. It felt like another planet, a planet of the lost. I was starting a new life again, for the third time in my short time on this earth.

As we drove through the dark streets I had no inkling of just how far my journey would eventually lead me. We passed shacks and tin-fronted commercial buildings, vast empty markets with wooden stalls and the cheap rubbish of Sudanese commerce scattered on the ground. There was no one in sight. At one point I panicked, thinking I didn't really want to go to London. I looked over to my mother and almost cried but that would not do. I put my face to the window so the breeze would cool my feverishness. The hot wind offered no relief. It was 105 degrees outside, down from 110 in the daytime. Dust still hung in the air from the most recent storm. It rarely rained in Khartoum. We just had haboobs, with their great clouds of choking sand and red dust. By the time we reached the airport the windscreen was streaked with dirt. My skin and clothes were dusty.

Athieng and I carried almost nothing, other than our family's hopes for our future. As I hugged everyone goodbye my brother Mayen said, 'Alek, do not lose your passport or this ticket. You won't get to London without them. They'll send you back here.'

The Sudan was the country of my ancestors, the soil where our cattle grazed, the land where our spirits lived, but I had no desire to return.

Now I was officially a refugee, with only a small bag, a passport, a ticket and a little bit of money.

I was fleeing a place where soldiers, militias and rebels killed each other and anyone – men, women or children – who got

in between them and their quest for power. I'd seen enough
dead bodies, like the ones that went putrid in the field by the
well where I used to gather water back in Wau. I didn't want to
see any more corpses, or become one myself.

At the gate Athieng and I said our final goodbyes.

'I'll see you in a few months, Mother,' I said.

Clutching our documents as if they were jewels, I shooed
my little sister ahead of me.

'Tickets and passport please,' the flight attendant said to me.

'No,' I said. 'These are mine.'

'What?'

'My brother told me not to lose these.'

'I just need to see them for a second.'

I was afraid she'd take them and never give them back, but
in the end I handed them over. She looked me up and down
like I was a country girl, which, in a way, I was. I didn't know
much about international flights, passports and the like.

The flight attendants tried to make us feel right at home.
They brought us croissants, but Athieng and I weren't used to
that kind of food and we got stomach cramps. When I went to
the bathroom I realised that there was something else I didn't
know anything about. The loo might as well have been a sci-
entific laboratory, for all I knew. It was a complete mystery. I'd
seen perhaps two flush toilets in my whole life, so I understood
the concept, but – my God – I didn't understand the layout.
Where was the flush? The directions were in English, not
Arabic, so I couldn't read them at all. And the paper – at home
we always used newspaper or leaves. I wasn't used to this fine
tissue. I was too embarrassed to ask for help but I was desperate, and also worried about my sister who was sitting by

herself. Finally, to my relief, a flight attendant showed me what to do.

For the rest of the night I sat in my seat, wide awake, looking out the window at the light on the wing as we flew through the deep darkness. I thought about Ajok and how I hadn't seen her in so long. I thought about the possibilities for my future. It was going to be so different from my past.

We landed at Frankfurt and changed onto our connecting flight. When we got off the plane the cool air frightened me. I'd never experienced anything like it. I was wearing only my Khartoum heatwave clothes, with nothing to keep me warm. A stewardess took us to our next flight, which we never would have found otherwise: the airport was vast, and we only spoke Dinka and Arabic. When we landed in London they brought steps to the plane and we walked down them into the wet, chilly air. I hadn't a clue about what we were supposed to do. So Athieng and I followed everyone onto a bus. I feared we'd done the wrong thing. It terrified me but I didn't show it because I didn't want to scare my sister. At immigration everyone was white. I hadn't known that there were so many white people on the planet. The officers showed us into a room where my sister was waiting, overcome with emotion. She hadn't seen her family for so many years.

Outside, as we walked for the train, the air felt like ice.

'But it's June,' I said. 'I thought it was supposed to be warm.'

'In England, this is warm,' my sister said, laughing.

'I'm not used to freezing.'

'You'll get used to it.'

We caught the train into the city and I sat and stared, soaking it all in. I couldn't believe how high up the train was running, on elevated tracks. The people were really strange.

All of a sudden a man got on carrying his bicycle, wearing tight trousers and a tight shirt. I felt embarrassed for him. How could he walk around like that? Everything was just so different from the Sudan. And also so different from what I'd expected.

At home, when I'd see pictures of Europe and America in magazines everything looked the same: the people, the buildings. Everything was so unusual I couldn't really see the differences between, say, England and Italy. It was all just clean, luxurious and strange, and full of abundance.

On the train it hit me that my thoughts about England had been way off target. I could see, just on the short journey from the airport, that some parts of the city were rough, with crumbling buildings and broken streetlights, while others were cleaner, more orderly, rich. It dawned on me that this was also what happened to Westerners when they thought about Africa. Their ideas were based mostly on pictures they'd seen. They assumed all of the countries were the same. They saw us all as poor and illiterate villagers; they thought we were all out to kill each other; they thought we were all chewing *khat* and walking along dirt roads. They didn't see our individuality.

It was exciting to look out of the train window. There were hundreds of advertisements. I didn't think about the models that had posed for these photographs because I was too busy trying to figure out what the pictures were selling. It certainly never occurred to me that one day I would be up there too.

My sister lived in a third-floor flat. Athieng and I were amazed to be living so high up and, that first night, spent a lot of time just staring out the windows, taking in the view of the streets below. When I wasn't doing that I was looking around the flat at the heaters, the stove, the sink, the bathroom. I spent

123

a lot of time in the bathroom, which seemed so luxurious to me. I'd wash my hands slowly; take a bath in hot water. I just couldn't believe it.

I was so happy to be with my sister. She cooked a stew and Athieng and I ate it with her, her husband, and our nieces and nephews. After a couple of days' rest I wanted to start helping out the family so I volunteered to go shopping. My sister gave me twenty pounds and sent my little nieces and nephews to help me buy food. By this time I'd taken to calling them 'the little terrors', because sometimes they could be so unruly, like any kids can, but we adored being around each other.

I was stunned when we walked up to this supermarket and saw all the provisions. I hesitated to go in because in the Sudan you wouldn't think of entering a store. Most of them were just little houses with a window. You'd go up to the window and say, 'I'd like some soap, please,' and they'd give it to you. 'It's OK, Auntie, we can just walk in there and pick out our stuff,' said my nephew.

I walked in there and thought, This is unreal – there is so much to choose from! I didn't understand why anyone could need so much. I just wanted okra and onions, but all of a sudden there were seven or eight different kinds of onions. Different kinds of celery. A whole row of chocolates. I'd only had chocolates about once a year, on special holidays, and here was a whole section devoted to them! I had to tell myself to focus, to calm down. I said to myself, Alek, this is your world now. You've got to learn.

We found what we needed and my nephews showed me the checkout. I'd been so overwhelmed by all the choices and somehow had lost the twenty-pound note my sister had given me. I was so embarrassed, and also terrified of what my sister would say when we got home. But she didn't shout or hit me or anything. She just said to be more careful next time.

I ran into the room Athieng and I shared and told her what I'd seen.

'Chocolates piled as high as a doorway!' I said. 'You wouldn't believe it.' Her eyes lit up, but she was too scared to come back to the supermarket with me.

The food in England blew my mind. I loved eating three times a day. I loved the lunches they served at my school. There would usually be a choice of a meat pie or a vegetarian dish, along with chips on the side, and boxes of juice to drink. A lot of the kids at that school weren't satisfied with that, though, so they'd go out to fast food restaurants for lunch. That made me think that the English children were rather spoilt. They couldn't make me out too well either. Of course, I looked different. The used to call me 'Midnight Black' because I'm so dark. They would be laughing at me about everything, even though a lot of them were from African families who grew up in England. They weren't all native English people, but they all spoke English, which I had to learn quickly.

The school placed Athieng and me in the normal classes. Fortunately, though, they gave each of us an assistant teacher to help us. My teacher was a real gem and I was soon talking and reading. I was studying English literature before I ever even heard of Shakespeare. I found maths challenging but I was eager to learn and to take advantage of the opportunities I was being granted.

In the beginning, the kids teased me about my scaly skin, which, admittedly, did make me look like a lizard. Amazingly, within three weeks of arriving in London my psoriasis, which had plagued me since I was a baby, just started to disappear. Every day I would stand in front of the mirror and look at my face. I almost couldn't believe what I was seeing – my skin was getting smoother. My legs cleared up. After a few months it had gone completely. Some doctors have told me it was due to the change in weather, from dry Sudan to wet England. Others have said it's because many of the stresses in my life disappeared. It also could have been because I went through puberty at that time.

It was hard to go to a strange city as a teenager. I had a few friends – maybe two – but mostly I felt isolated. While the other people in my class were going to parties, I was at home babysitting.

I felt less awkward once my skin cleared up. It became easier to make friends. There weren't many Sudanese in England at the time – not anything like the twenty thousand or so who live there now – but my family knew some of them and there was a good community. If one person got married, all of us exiles would go to the party. I made friends with some of the girls and my older sister, who watched me like a hawk, trusted that they wouldn't get me in trouble. The Sudanese girls understood what I was going through and taught me the ways of London.

Not that I got out that much. My sister and her husband had four children, two girls named Aman and Awut, and two boys named Lual and Tong, and they both worked nights, my sister at a hotel and her husband as a security guard. They needed me to help. I'd come home from school, make dinner for the children and look after them. They were family, but they were anything but easy. When I tried to get them to do chores, such as clear their dishes from the table or clean their rooms, they'd threaten to tell their mother that I hit them. Sometimes they'd just walk away from me while I was talking to them. It was mentally and emotionally exhausting. I was just fourteen years old. My sister needed me, so I didn't complain.

In addition to the stress of adapting to life in a new city it was becoming clear that my mother wasn't going to get out of the Sudan for a long while. It was hard to get the necessary papers, and even harder to get the money. She didn't have a telephone and there was no reliable mail service in the country. The only way we could communicate with her was by sending messages via our friend who worked in a fancy hotel in Khartoum, through whom my sister had been sending money.

Soon I started feeling bad about eating my sister's food and living in her house without contributing any money to help her, or my mother, so I took a job working mornings and weekends stacking shelves in a supermarket. I was the lowest worker there, and one day the floor manager played a joke on me. He gave me a T-shirt that said 'Staff Chief' on the front. I didn't understand the joke, and when the boss saw that he got angry and said, 'Why are you wearing that shirt?' About a year later they did put me in charge of people, and I got the shirt back.

After that job I worked at a photocopy shop for a while, which taught me to keep things neat and I also learned how to use a computer. I was sixteen by then and at about that time my mother escaped the Sudan, along with two more of my brothers and sisters. I was delighted to see her, after three years without so much as a word on the telephone.

She seemed well, and surprised to see how much I'd changed. My English was good, so she relied on me for that. Athieng moved in with her but I stayed with Ajok for a while to help her with the children. I was sad not to live with my mother but my sister needed me. Finally, after about a year, I left my sister and at last moved in with my mother.

It was great to have so many family members around. Sadly, my brother Mayen and my sister Adaw were by then in their twenties and so could not be included in the family's application for a refugee visa along with the other children. When Mayen applied on his own he was refused. He had to stay in Khartoum and, since the government knew his family had fled, the police persecuted him for being part of a family of 'traitors'. I know it was dreadful for him, although he's never talked about it. They weren't as hard on Adaw. Years later Mayen and Adaw made it to Canada.

My mother settled in quite well, although it was harder for her to adjust, given that she was fully grown. She met a number of other Sudanese women and they became firm friends. They shared their feelings and experiences in ways that they wouldn't have been able to do with English people or immigrants from other countries. My mother felt less lonely with these other women around, many of whom had also lost their husbands in the Sudan.

They even recreated many of their African customs. I was surprised when they figured out how to make dried okra. I mean, England isn't famous for its bright sunlight. They devised a method of drying it slowly above the stove. I was so happy to have dried okra again, after being away from the Sudan for so long. I tried serving it to my nephews and nieces, who'd never set foot in Africa. They turned up their noses.

'Auntie, what's that?'

'Dried okra stew.'

'Oh no, we don't like it,' one of them said. 'We won't eat that.'

'OK. But you don't know what you're missing.'

During my last year of school my class was taken to visit various universities, including Oxford and Cambridge. It was during our visit to the London Institute that I suddenly realised that I knew exactly what I wanted to do. I'd always drawn pictures or made little sculptures out of clay and here I saw people who were devoting their lives to making art. That touched something deep in my heart, and I decided to apply. My mother didn't really understand why I would want to study art instead of medicine or finance, or any of the other fields that immigrants usually push their children into, but she didn't interfere.

I was accepted into the London Institute with a scholarship and started classes in 1994. It was such a fantastic place. I loved painting and would spend hours every day working in the studio. I also started taking singing lessons at night. My family approved: if I'd asked to go out to a club, they'd have said no, but since I'd found a hobby they were more comfortable with me being independent. It wasn't like I was hanging out in South London at all hours, but still, it was a chance to get out.

I needed some way to pay for my art supplies, which were expensive, so I took a job at the BBC, which sounds great, except that I was cleaning toilets. Every morning I'd get up at four o'clock and get ready for work. My bedroom never seemed to warm up, even when the heating was on, so it would be freezing in the early morning. I hated getting out of

129

bed to scrub toilets. I had to be disciplined. By then I understood that if I wanted something I had to go and get it myself.
That job was my trust fund. But that doesn't mean I liked it.

Some days I'd walk into the toilets and think, My God, how
can anyone be so filthy? You would not believe how dirty they
got. The supervisor was a mean woman who'd scowl at me as
if I were worth less than nothing. Once I'd finished my shift I'd
go to college for the day, then come home to take care of my
sister's kids. Finally, one cold morning I said to myself, 'I can't
take this any more,' and quit my job.

I found a new job, working in a hair salon. I would get
coffee and tea for the customers, sweep up the hair and lug
supplies up from the basement. The owner was a cockney man
with a heavy accent and the tough attitude of a guy who'd
fought for everything he had.

'This will be brilliant,' he said when he hired me. 'I'm really
glad you're working here.'

He appreciated hard workers like me. Maybe he saw some
of himself in me, a little Dinka girl who came to London,
taught herself English and got into art school. After all, he'd
grown up in the East End and worked his way up. Now
wealthy people would fly him out to Los Angeles or New
York, just to cut their hair. But, in truth, given how English
society works, no matter how rich he got he'd always be a seen
as a cockney. Just as some people would always see me as nothing more than a backward African girl, no matter what I did
with my life.

I never spoke much at the salon and the other employees
didn't really know how I'd ended up in London. Some of
customers spoke Arabic and a few times I heard them gossip-
ing about me: 'Who is that skinny girl, anyway? She brought

130

me tea with a hair in it.' They got the shock of their lives when I replied, in Arabic, 'Don't you speak about me that way.' Soon I was promoted to shampoo girl, which was, at times, disgusting: some of the women had the filthiest hair I'd ever seen. But it was a job, and it was a step up from cleaning toilets.

My mother was very strict with me and didn't like me to go to parties. Of course, I didn't have any boyfriends. She wouldn't have allowed that at all. I did have one good friend, an English girl who I'd met at school.

I remember my friend once said to me, 'So your mother won't let you go out with boys? She won't let you go to parties? You can't do anything?'

I thought she was criticising me and I became very defensive about it. Later I realised that actually she was saying how it was wonderful that my mother watched over me. My friend's parents weren't like that at all. Her mother was from Singapore and her father was Indian, and so she was really beautiful. She was also really bright, so you'd think she had everything going for her. Her parents were divorced, and preoccupied with their own issues, so really she had to raise herself, without any guidance. I think that filled her with a sadness that influenced every area of her life. Even when she was having fun there was a sad part of her that she had to hold back.

We'd have such laughs together. I understood her, and she understood me, and we adapted our friendship to each other in a really beautiful way. She always gave me the best advice.

One weekend in 1995 she invited me to join her on a visit to Crystal Palace Park in South London, where one of the local radio stations was hosting a street fair. We took the bus there and were walking around, thinking about getting a hot dog or some candyfloss, when all of a sudden a short, blonde woman walked over to me and said, 'Have you ever thought about being a model?' Embarrassed, I blushed – she probably couldn't see it because my skin is so dark, but I tell you, I was turning red. My friend looked shocked. We always thought she was the pretty one, not me. 'Here's my card,' she said. 'I really think you should come in and see us. I'd like you to meet Nigel – he's an agent I work with.'

'I don't know if my mother would let me,' I said.

'Well, I think you'd be really good. I'm serious. Do you mind if I take a snapshot?'

She took my picture and as she walked away she mimed holding a phone to her ear and mouthed, 'Call me.'

I almost melted, right there in Crystal Palace Park.

'Wow, what do you think?' I said.

I didn't know the first thing about modelling, but my friend looked at the card, which said 'Models 1'.

'This is a super agency! This is brilliant!'

'What do they do?'

'They turn you into a supermodel.'

'What?'

'A supermodel, Alek. She's going to put you on the covers of magazines. You could be in adverts.'

For a second I could see myself on the television. Oh, that would be nice. But I didn't say it.

'That's ridiculous,' I said. 'Me?'

I'd never imagined being a model. I didn't even know they existed before I arrived in London, I thought as I paid for some candyfloss for both of us. Later, as I said goodbye to my friend, she gave me a strange look.

'You aren't going to call her, are you?'

'Well . . .'

'If you don't call her I will kill you dead, and then I'll kill you again,' she said. 'You're crazy, Alek.'

'I'll check with my mother.'

I went home and told her what had happened. She just gave me a look that said: don't be a fool. Stay in college. Get your work done and don't think ridiculous thoughts.

I was an emotional wreck. My friend had raised my hopes and now my mother was dashing them, though I knew I'd rather listen to my mother than anyone else. Even though she was strict I knew she'd never want anything bad for me.

I went back to school. I worked at the salon. I watched my nieces and nephews and, as always, I behaved like a good Dinka girl. I put the card in my bedside drawer and never called the agency. It just wasn't meant to be.

Two weeks later my mother said that the scout from the agency had called. They wanted me to go down to their offices. I could see that my mother had softened somewhat. She wouldn't tell me to do it, but she wasn't exactly telling me not to do it.

Then the phone rang again. It was the scout.

'What happened?' she said. 'I thought you were coming by.'

It wasn't often that a girl got scouted and didn't follow it up.

'Are you really serious?' I said.

'I'm serious, Alek. I think you could do very, very well,' she said in her cut-glass accent, which I loved.

So I said to my sister, 'Let's go and see.' We went to the offices and sat on nice leather chairs in the waiting area. Magazine covers from *Elle* and *Vogue* were all over the walls. I went from being curious, to being excited, to thinking, Look at all these girls, these famous models – are you sure I should be here? Reading my mind, my sister took control, 'Alek, calm down.'

The scout came out and took us into a large room with a round table surrounded by chairs. My palms were sweating and my heart was beating fast. Then a man came in, handsome, about forty years old.

'Alek, it's such a pleasure to meet you,' he said in a brilliant Scottish accent. 'I'd like to represent you.'

That's when it all started to become real. He said that he wanted to put together some test shots to start sending me out on 'go-sees' – a term I'd never heard, which he picked up from my blank expression.

'For advertisements,' he explained. 'On television.'

I was shocked.

'Me? On TV?'

'We've got to get a book of your photos together, and then build it up with some work. Then you're going to have a career.'

I looked at my sister and she looked at me. Suddenly, the Sudan, with its haboobs and boy soldiers, seemed very far away.

'When do you want to start?' Nigel asked. 'We'll get going with ads, magazines . . .'

I left their offices with a hundred crazy thoughts in my head. Should I or shouldn't I? Was the agency real or were they trying to trick me? Could I be a famous model? Probably not, but what did I have to lose? I was sick of babysitting every night and washing old ladies' hair at the weekends. A few days later, with my mother's blessing, I told Nigel that I was ready to start. He turned out to be wonderful. He was down to earth and not too pushy, and he had that great accent. I couldn't have been happier.

All of a sudden I was a model, although I definitely wasn't an overnight success. I was still going to school, still watching my nieces and nephews at night, still washing old ladies' hair at the weekend. But now my agent would call and tell me that I had to see a photographer who thought he could use me. It was a surreal life. There I was, a girl from a little town in the Sudan. I had spent most of my life covered with psoriasis, which is not the prettiest disease, and definitely not what you'd expect from a cover girl. Now I was in the heart of London with people interested in my 'look' and photographers wanting to take pictures of me. Yet no matter what my agent would say, no matter how flattering the photographer might be, I'd still go home to my mother's house to eat okra and talk Dinka.

It wasn't long before I decided to tell my boss that I couldn't work at his salon any more. But he wouldn't let me quit; he kept convincing me to stay. I found that flattering and didn't want to hurt his feelings but I just didn't want to work there any more. In the end I came up with a little lie to help me out. One Saturday morning I wrapped bandages around my ankle, hobbled into the salon and told him that I'd sprained it. He looked me up and down with some suspicion.

'That's OK,' he said. 'I won't make you go up and down the stairs any more. You can stay up here with me.'

No, I thought. My ploy had gone a little wrong.

I limped over to him and said, 'I can't work with this knee.'

'I thought you said it was your ankle.'

'My ankle, right. I can't work on it.'

'Well then, come back when it gets better.'

I limped away, feeling guilty for lying. Once I was down the street, out of sight, I unwrapped my foot and jumped for joy.

I didn't go back to the salon until years later, when I had my driver stop as we were passing by. I went inside and said hello.

'Alek, look at you!' he said, greeting me warmly.

I told him the truth, that I'd lied to him before.

'Hey, don't worry about that,' he said. 'You're a super-model!'

CHAPTER 8

The children at school in London had made fun of me for having such long legs, for having such dark skin, for having a round, African face and short, reddish hair. Everything. It was therefore quite a surprise to become a fashion model. After all, I was the girl who'd been covered with lizard-like skin for most of her life. But the agency wanted me, and I wasn't going to argue with that.

My mother had different ideas. In the Sudan we just didn't see that much media, other than television once in a while. I'd never really considered that I could make money from my looks, and my mother had thought about it even less than me. All she knew about women who posed for pictures was that they were generally up to no good.

We were standing in the kitchen one afternoon, the smell of beef stew filling the flat, when I told her I had a job the next day, posing for an editorial in a magazine. Her face twisted up.

'And what will you be doing?'

I could tell she was picturing some man taking advantage of me, talking her little girl into taking her clothes off for the camera, or worse.

'It's a story on dresses,' I said. 'New dresses.'

'And you're sure you'll be wearing those dresses?'

'Mother,' I said.

'Don't "Mother" me. You don't know what these people can be like.'

'My agent set it up. She's not going to do anything bad.'

'What is an agent but someone who makes money off you?'

'It's legitimate,' I said. 'And I'm not stupid. I won't do anything that I wouldn't think you would approve of.'

She was silent for a moment. She looked into my eyes and her face softened.

'Of course you won't, precious,' she said. 'You're a smart girl, and you're right. I trust you. Just be careful.'

But I could see behind her eyes. She was thinking that I would end up on Page Three. My mother was worried that I'd end up taking my clothes off and putting myself in bad situations. It's very much to her credit that she didn't just lock me in the closet and throw away the key until this whole modelling thing passed.

My very first assignment was a portrait test with a photographer named Mark Mattock. I did it for free, of course, since I was new, but two of the images were later published in *Vibe*, an influential New York music magazine, and that got other people interested in me. For instance, a casting director thought I'd be perfect for the video of Tina Turner's theme song for the James Bond film *GoldenEye*. That was the first of many times that I was cast because of, not in spite of, my African features – they wanted someone 'exotic' who lived in a jungle.

138

I met Tina, but I didn't get to hang out with her or anything. That video was a lesson in how complex the industry can be. They had me posing in a leopard-print bikini and high leather boots, with wild tribal make-up, in a dark room while lights flashed across my body. I was thinking, maybe my mother was right, maybe I am just being exploited. It turned out well after all: in the final video I'm an elusive, dark, exotic creature who appears for about ten seconds, if that. It's not a nudie show, but people noticed and I started to get more work.

Then the creative director of *i-D* magazine hired me to pose for a Burger King advertisement he was styling. He must have liked me, because he mentioned me to other people in the business.

This was a lot better than scrubbing toilets at the BBC! I didn't mind the pay at all, which could be hundreds of pounds a day. When I worked I earned at least as much as I did in my other, less glamorous jobs. The problem was that the work was irregular.

Models are paid by the job. The highest-paid work is when you are under contract to a certain beauty or fashion product and you become the 'face' of that company. Those contracts can pay millions of dollars a year. Then there is the catwalk work, which can pay anywhere from five hundred dollars a day to tens of thousands of dollars, all for about five hours of work. Often a model can do several catwalk shows in a day.

When a model is hired by the day for an advertising job, as opposed to having a contract, she'll get the same rates as cat-walk work, and often these jobs last three or four days. Modelling for television also pays the same, but there's even more money to be made if your agent negotiates a royalty, so that you receive a fee every time an advertisement airs. It's a crazy business and the models' wages seem really high, until you discover that these days the top fashion photographers can easily earn upwards of 125,000 dollars per day. So, really, models aren't even near the top of the heap.

The pinnacle is very narrow: only a very small group of models, photographers, fashion stylists, make-up artists and hair stylists make it. To earn the top money they've got to keep themselves in the public eye, as well as being on the very cutting edge. That means they have to produce fashion spreads for magazines that are much more creative and risky than anything they might do in advertising jobs for corporations. It's a game, really, where the corporations only want to hire super-creative and edgy people for their campaigns, but then don't really want to be too outrageous, as they still need to sell their product.

The result is that the creative teams and models must do 'cool' work in magazine editorials in order to keep their credibility, so that they can attract the lucrative work offered by advertisers. Since magazines such as *Vogue*, *Elle* and *Harper's Bazaar* don't have the bottomless pockets of companies like Hermès, they – relatively – don't pay much at all. Models, make-up artists and even photographers will do editorial work that pays as little as 150 dollars a day, knowing that if it has an edge it will help them earn money in the future.

These jobs are also good for new models that want to establish names for themselves. In my first few months, the only jobs I got were editorials, or photographer's tests that I'd do in exchange for a little bit of money, if I was lucky, and sheets of photos that my agency could use to build up my book. This was the portfolio – essentially a photo album – that they'd circulate to photographers looking for new models.

The thing about modelling is that you can become very well known very quickly. Just as there was a bush telegraph back in the villages of the Sudan, there's a fashion telegraph. A stylist will see a new girl and spread the word to a make-up artist who'll tell a casting director who'll tell a photographer who'll tell a magazine editor and pretty soon your name will be buzzing back and forth across the Atlantic. I was lucky enough to have that happen to me early on. It didn't translate into big money, because I was still a black African model and advertisers didn't think their consumers would respond well to that image, but the people who made the images – the stylists and the photographers – liked my look.

One day, about six months after I'd done my first test, my agent called with a trembling voice to say that a photographer, Richard Avedon, wanted to shoot me in New York for something called the Pirelli Calendar. I thought going to New York would be pretty exciting, since I'd never been anywhere other than the Sudan and London.

They gave me my tickets and I headed out to the airport. Since I hadn't flown anywhere after arriving in London from Khartoum, I had a little trouble navigating the airport. I eventually made it to the check-in desk, but when I handed over my ticket they made a face.

In order to be admitted to England as a refugee I'd had to surrender my Sudanese passport to the British authorities and take something called a United Kingdom Travel Document. It's much thicker than a passport and the cover is blue with black writing, as opposed to the standard maroon British passport. It really stands out and, to me, looked suspicious. Also, I hadn't travelled to any other countries since arriving in

England and so didn't know that holders of Travel Documents were required to get an exit visa.

The officials told me that I couldn't travel without that. So I ran to a pay phone and called my agent. He wasn't in. I wasn't able to get my papers in time for the shoot, which was to take place the next morning. So I missed it.

Later, I was shocked to find out that Richard Avedon was perhaps the most famous and respected fashion photographer in the world, a man who'd been shooting portraits since the 1940s and who had produced brilliant journalistic books with writers such as James Baldwin and Truman Capote. What a missed opportunity! Then, when I learned that the Pirelli Calendar featured movie stars and top models and was one of the most coveted jobs a model could get, I had to sit down and collect my thoughts. Not so much because I had missed it, but because this great photographer and incredible publication had decided that I was good enough. It was a total affirmation of my career. In 1999, when I was shot for Pirelli by Herb Ritts, I thought about Avedon. What a way to start a career – by blowing a job with him! After the Avedon fiasco, nothing much happened for a while. The work was so irregular that I couldn't predict how much I'd earn, but I still had my expenses. My art supplies for school were outrageously high priced, but I had no choice but to buy them. I also needed to contribute to rent and food at home. I had to find part-time jobs, as well as going to art school and, in the evenings, I babysat my sister's children.

In between all this, if I got a booking or a go-see I'd have to rearrange my complex schedule, sometimes missing classes or getting a friend to cover for me at work. I never knew what to expect when I arrived at the studio. I remember one shoot, for

The Face, where the photographer had me wear a black rubber clothes and a mask and prance around the studio like Dracula. If my mother had known about that she would have stopped me modelling immediately!

I really wanted to do well as a model, and my agent was a great support. He really believed in me, although after nine months of doing shoots and go-sees, my career wasn't going as well as I'd hoped. I needed money and, frankly, I was exhausted by all the running around. Yes, my agent was telling me that everything was going swimmingly, but he wasn't living my life. I found it a real struggle and the glamour of being a model was quickly wearing off. I called him to schedule a meeting.

On the bus over to the agency I rehearsed my monologue: 'I've been very happy working as a model, and you have been great in terms of encouraging me. I really appreciate that, but I don't think I can continue working in this piecemeal way, never knowing how much I'm going to earn from one week to the next. I need stability. So, unless you're able to guarantee me a monthly salary, I will have to stop modelling. It's just a matter of practicality.'

Of course, by the time I sat down in the conference room with my agent, his assistant and a couple of other people, I was feeling rather nervous and my well-rehearsed speech came out as more of plea than a demand. Nonetheless, I got my point across. They were shocked. And I was shocked at how shocked they were.

'Alek, do you realise that no other girl has ever asked us to do anything of the kind?'

I said no, but I also said that I wasn't any other girl. I was me. And I was having trouble with the way things were going.

I now know that it was to my great advantage that I'd never been desperate to be a model. It was never something I dreamed of, so the thought of failing at it didn't really bother me.

'Alek, you know you've had an amazing career already,' said my agent, mentioning Avedon, Tina Turner and *Vibe*. 'We see you doing lots of television work, getting contracts with the big cosmetic companies in the future. We see you getting billboards. Magazine spreads. It just takes time. It would be very unusual, to say the least, for an agency like us to guarantee you a certain level of income before your career is established. We really love you, but I don't think we could do that.'

I told them that, in which case, I was going to stop being a model. I don't think they believed me at first, but then I walked out and didn't get in touch with them again. I felt okay with it – life goes on.

I guess they didn't feel okay with it as a few weeks after I quit the agency my agent invited me in for a meeting. He told me that, because they saw so much potential in me, they were going to make an exception. They guaranteed me enough money to live on. Just a few hundred pounds a month, but it enabled me to quit my other menial jobs.

My agent also told me that he thought it was time for me to go to New York. Wow, I thought as I walked to the bus. New York?

My mother was pretty impressed that I was going to New York, and didn't show that she was worried. She trusted me to do the right thing. She'd sent me across the world by myself before, although this time there was no one at the other end to protect me, except for the agent in New York, from the Ford

Agency, who would be representing me in the States. Despite her blessing, I didn't make it far on my first attempt: my agency hadn't worked things out for me. I decided I'd never entrust that sort of thing to anyone again.

A couple of days later I'd straightened everything out. Descending into JFK was an incredible experience. I thought I'd seen everything, after living in London, but clearly New York was on a whole different level. After we landed I grabbed my small carry-on bag, with just about enough clothes and stuff for three or four days, and headed off. The immigration officials had other ideas. They took one look at my refugee passport and dragged me off to a holding room, where they questioned me.

'What is the purpose of your visit to New York?'

'I am a model.'

The man gave me a quizzical look.

'A model?'

I guess I didn't look much like the supermodels of the day.

They took my fingerprints and photographed me. The officers were cold and unhelpful; I was frightened. After two hours they finally let me go. The airport was a chaotic mess that reminded me much more of Africa than tidy London. I hailed a yellow taxi and set off into the New York evening, towards East Sixth Street and Avenue B, where the agency was putting me up in a 'models' apartment' with some other wannabes.

Approaching Manhattan, I couldn't believe the size of the skyscrapers: the World Trade Center, the Empire State and Chrysler buildings formed a twinkling dreamscape against the setting sun. The second the taxi rose out of the midtown tunnel I felt as if I'd entered a jungle of sorts. The summer air

145

was hot and wet and strange sounds came out of doorways, cars and people's stereos. I started to get nervous, breathing heavily. I didn't want anyone to see the sweat stains on my shirt. I wiped my forehead with my sleeve.

A young woman was looking out the window of the apartment building when I arrived.

'Alek, you made it!' she called. 'Come right up.'

She seemed friendly, but my heart was beating fast when I got out of the taxi. I said to myself, 'What on earth have I got myself into?' She buzzed me through the door and welcomed me to the apartment. Her name was Mora Rowe, and she was the agent assigned to look after the girls. She was going to become one of my most cherished friends in the world, but at the time she seemed like a particularly excited alien, greeting me with a big smile and the craziest Californian accent I'd ever heard.

'Like, wow, you're here,' she said. 'I'm, like, so glad to see you.'

Her enthusiasm was infectious.

There were two other girls in the apartment. I took the centre room, which only had a skylight, because it was more private than the other rooms. I didn't mind the lack of windows – I'd certainly seen worse on my travels.

On my first day in New York I walked out of the models' apartment into the street and felt the full force of New York blow right over me. The apartment was in the East Village, which, at the time, was still quite rough in places. I turned left out of the apartment and headed east, which was generally seen as a risky proposition. A man brushed past me and stared right into my eyes, then moved his gaze up and down my body like I was for sale in a market. So brazen! That just didn't happen in London. At the corner a huge spray-painted mural honoured someone called Tyron. His face was painted on the wall, festooned with flowers and crosses. He died when he was just seventeen. Why? I wondered.

Further down the block I came across two young men injecting each other with drugs. I'd heard that people did this, but I'd never seen it in London. Believe it or not, one of them whistled affectionately at me as I passed, the needle still dangling from his vein. I decided this really wasn't for me so I went around the block and walked in the other direction. I heard such a mix of music on that walk: salsa, reggae, even Fela Kuti, the famous Nigerian musician. The streets were filled with people selling used clothes, cassettes and CDs, books, jewellery, anything you could imagine. I loved it.

That night, Mora wanted to take me out.

'Like, put this on,' she said, handing me a colourful sarong. 'We're going down to Puerto Rican world.'

I had no idea what a Puerto Rican was, but she made them sound very exotic. We walked down to the Lower East Side. It was a hot night and there were a lot of people in the streets, some of them dancing to salsa music. It was all really festive and I kept saying, 'Are they Puerto Rican? Is he Puerto Rican?'

Mora just laughed. In time I learned that half the people in my neighbourhood were actually Puerto Rican. They were just New Yorkers like everyone else.

We went to a little Mexican restaurant at the corner of Stanton Street and Ludlow Street. It was such a funky place, with all kinds of friendly people. The conversation flowed; Mora and I flirted with a couple of men and had a really good time. That was quite an experience for me, because I was still very inexperienced and naive about men.

I went back to the models' apartment feeling very positive, with great hope for the future.

In the morning Mora gave me some subway tokens and showed me how to get to my first go-see. I was worried that my clothes weren't good enough. I was wearing some old jeans my sister had given me. She'd bought them second-hand at a market in London.

'Oh my God,' said Mora. 'Where did you get those vintage Wranglers? They're unbelievable!'

That made me feel pretty good. In fact, those jeans got me a lot of comments those first few months in New York. One woman offered me two hundred bucks for them. I was wondering, What is this strange world I've entered?

I went to the subway and somehow found my way uptown to the address Mora had given me. I entered the dingy hallway and climbed three flights of dirty stairs to the office of an advertising casting agency. A middle-aged woman sat at a little desk. She snapped her gum at me, grabbed my 'look book' and gave it a quick once-over. Then handed it back to me. She looked down at her desk and kept working. I stood there for a minute. I cleared my throat. She looked up.

'You're new, right?'

'Yes,' I said. 'You're my first go-see in New York.'

'Well, that's it. You're through here.'

'You don't need me?'

'Don't need you. You're not what we want.'

Whoa, I thought. This is brutal. How was I going to get used to this New York brusqueness?

Then she looked at me admiringly, which took me by surprise.

'Hey, where'd you get those Wranglers? Those are dope!'

I left on a high.

That evening I put the sarong on again, with a skimpy top I'd brought from London, and went out for a walk. This was the kind of outfit I could wear in London with no problem, but the East Village was a whole different story. There were groups of young muscular guys on most of the corners, wearing vests and bandanas, big sneakers and gold chains. They liked the way I looked.

'Hey, what's holding that skirt up, girl?' one of them called out.

'Hey baby, did it hurt when you fell down from heaven?' said another.

I turned around and went home to hide in my room.

'What's wrong, Alek?' Mora asked me.

I told her I was still a virgin, that I'd never really had a boyfriend, and that I was shocked at the way the men in the city spoke to women on the street. I said they'd never do that in the Sudan or in London.

'That's just you in that sarong,' she said. 'With legs up here.'

The next time I went out I wore jeans, but I didn't really go out much at all. Instead, I liked to turn on the fan in my room and blow the dry heat around, telling myself, 'This is the weather of the Sudan.'

There was an ever-changing procession of girls coming in and out of the other rooms. Many of them would stay out all night long, night after night. I'd see them in the morning, hung over and looking rough. I would think, Thank God I got some sleep, because I've got a lot to do today, honey.

My days were filled with go-sees. Mora would give me a list of appointments in the morning, but more go-sees would come

in during the day. I'd run all over the city with my book –
sometimes to offices, sometimes to photographers' studios or
magazines. Sometimes I'd be there for less than two minutes
and other times they'd ask me to do a test photograph. I never
knew what to expect, except rejection. That seemed to be the
only consistent part of the experience.

At the time, supermodels with slender but curvy bodies and
long thick hair ruled. Most of them had fair skin and fair hair.
This look was what sold cosmetics, clothes, everything. The
advertisers were afraid to try anything else, and so were the magazines. Sure, Avedon had wanted me. But Middle America
didn't.

On the rare occasions when someone actually took the time
to talk to me I found it completely disorienting. I went on
these go-sees, sometimes sixteen of them in a single day, for
two weeks straight. Every night I'd return to the apartment
and cook some noodles or soup. Once in a while Mora would
make some Italian food, like spaghetti, and I loved that. For a
huge treat I'd buy a Chinese takeaway for a couple of dollars
from a place on the corner. Mostly I tried to save money as I
wasn't earning anything yet and had to depend on advances
from the agency to cover my rent and expenses. I didn't want
to get too far into debt.

Two hundred dollars would last me at least a month. I never
went to the cinema; I didn't go to museums. I bought just one
piece of clothing in that first year. I was walking down the
street wishing I could buy some more clothes. All of a sudden
I came across a junkie selling stuff from a blanket laid out on
the pavement. He had an amazing 1970s Rayon shirt with a
big pointed collar. I had to have it. 'Wow. I'll just take that
home and wash it,' I said.

He gave me a funny look, and I realised that I'd hurt his feelings by suggesting his clothes were dirty. He took my dollar anyway and I got my shirt, which felt very fancy. I still have that shirt – I'll never throw it away as I love it so much. Meanwhile, rather than go the launderette, I'd wash my underwear out by hand back at the models' apartment at night.

The people at the Ford agency definitely thought I had something special, but they weren't sure they could convince photographers and advertisers to take the risk of using such an 'exotic' creature as me. By 'exotic' they always meant black African. I was blacker than most and they seemed very scared of that. While the agency took some of the other girls in the apartment shopping for clothes they never offered that to me. I guess it was because they didn't want to risk losing their small investment. Still, Mora believed in me enough to send me out each day.

Nothing came of it and, eventually, the agency was discouraged. They just didn't think anyone was going to be interested. They told me to leave the models' apartment. I cried, feeling very disappointed that it had all come to nothing and I was going to go back to London. Mora, however, stuck by me. She even invited me to stay in her apartment in Brooklyn for a while. I moved out there and kept going on go-sees.

'You've just got to find the right person who understands your look and then you are going to be huge. I know it!' Mora said.

One day she sent me to a test shot on the roof of a building in SoHo for a new line being put out by François Nars. I'd never heard of him, even though he was a hugely successful

151

make-up artist. He said, 'I've heard about you. My friend at *i-D* magazine mentioned you.' That made me realise how connected people in fashion are, and how small the community is. Finding out that an editor in London had been promoting me started to make me feel a part of the fashion world. I put on a white T-shirt and Nars himself applied some deep red lipstick called 'Times Square' to my lips. That was all the preparation we did for that photo. He ended up using it in his ad campaign. Well, the Ford people were very pleased by that, and realised that yes, actually, people would use an African model as dark as me to sell make-up. That was a big coup, and suddenly they were more interested. An even bigger coup came a few weeks later when my agent got a call from Steven Meisel's office.

This photographer was famous, not least for the photos he took of Madonna for her book, *Sex*. He was the hottest thing going and shot regularly for American *Vogue* and lots of other magazines. He was well-known for seeking out the newest girls to shoot for his clients. He had made Linda Evangelista into a star. His call was clearly a big deal.

Suddenly, the people at Ford took an even greater interest in me. They sent me to the go-see with a male representative of the agency, who made a big fuss of buying expensive flowers to take to the meeting. I was embarrassed, because it's really not my style, but I was a new model, so there wasn't anything I could do about it.

It turned out that Meisel never sees the models on the go-see. Instead, his people took some Polaroids of me and sent me on my way. They didn't seem too impressed with the bouquet. Not long after, I was booked into a shoot for Italian *Vogue*, which is absolutely the most prestigious place for a model to

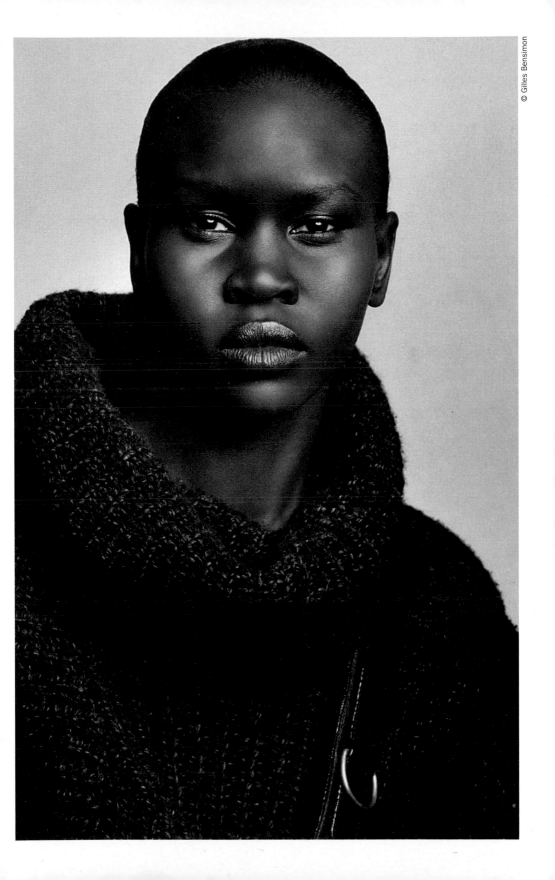

With my younger sister
Athieng, when I was 24.

This photograph of my left
hand was the inspiration for
several of my paintings. I hope
that the long life line that runs
across my palm is an accurate
predictor of the future.

I painted these sturdy flip-flops in 2000, while thinking of my life in the Sudan and the flimsy old flip-flops we always wore.

Soon after I bought my house in Brooklyn, I started painting again. This portrait of my late father, Athian Wek, was one of the first paintings I finished, in 2000. It was the first portrait I ever painted.

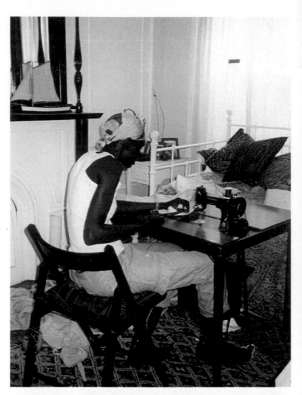

Right: A friend gave me this sewing machine, which I used to whip up my first bags at home in Brooklyn.

Bottom left: I was photographed with this silver Akua bag from my collection at one of my first trade shows.

Bottom right: This photograph, taken for British *Vogue*, shows me with a WEK1933 T-bag.

I wore this outlandish outfit for the Christian Dior haute couture show in 2004.

Backstage with Vivienne Westwood, just before her 2001 show in Paris.

It was such an honour to walk the catwalk as the 'bride'. With Karl Lagerfeld at one of his Chanel couture shows.

On the steps of my
house in Brooklyn.

An artist who goes by just one name, Eddie, projected my photos on this wall above Lafayette
Street, in SoHo, New York City, in 1998, and painted my portrait.

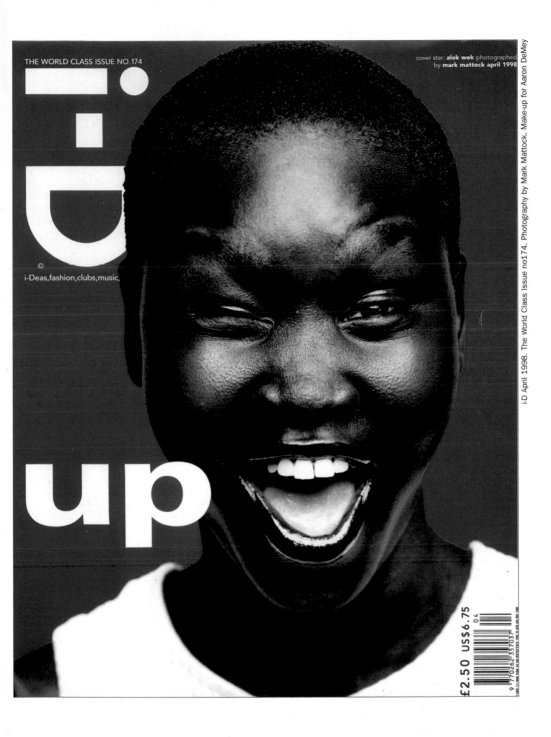

THE WORLD CLASS ISSUE NO.174

cover star: **alek wek** photographed
by **mark mattock** april 1998

i-D

©

i-Deas,fashion,clubs,music,

up

i-D April 1998. The World Class Issue no174. Photography by Mark Mattock. Make-up for Aaron DeMey

£2.50 US$6.75

04

9 770262 357037

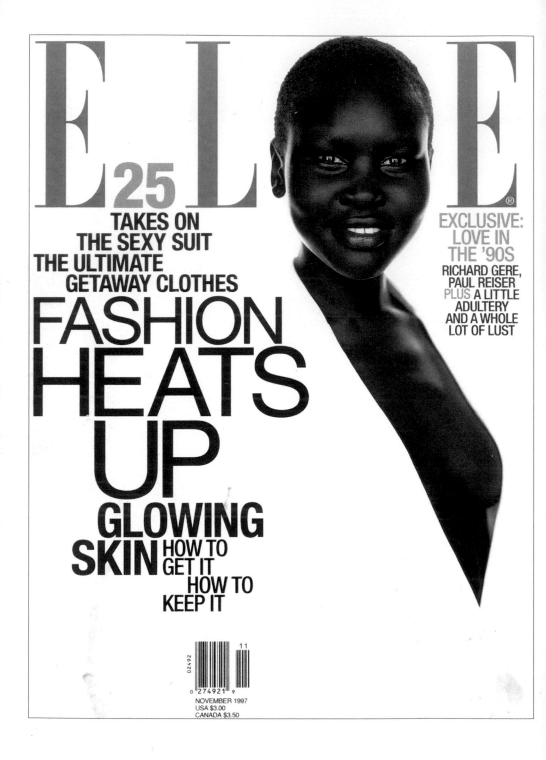

ELLE

25

TAKES ON THE SEXY SUIT

THE ULTIMATE GETAWAY CLOTHES

FASHION HEATS UP

GLOWING SKIN
HOW TO GET IT
HOW TO KEEP IT

EXCLUSIVE:
LOVE IN THE '90S

RICHARD GERE, PAUL REISER PLUS A LITTLE ADULTERY AND A WHOLE LOT OF LUST

NOVEMBER 1997
USA $3.00
CANADA $3.50

0 274921 9

11

02492

appear. And I was to be shot by Steven Meisel himself. It wasn't quite perfect, however.

'They think you're too fat,' Mora told me. 'They want you to slim down.'

What? All my life I'd been told I was too skinny. I'd nearly starved, literally, a few times over the years, yet they were telling me I was too fat? What was the world coming to? This definitely is the model's curse, and it's only worsened in recent years. No matter how thin you are someone always thinks you could be thinner. I've known so many models that have literally starved themselves for weeks at a time to prepare for the catwalk or photo shoots. It's always clear when someone is hungry for a long time, because they tend to become depressed and listless. I've felt that, not because I needed to fit into a dress, but because I was a refugee. I don't ever want to feel like that again.

'Really, don't worry about it,' Mora said. 'They think you could lose five pounds, but I think you're fine. You eat the right things; you exercise. You're still a teenager so don't sweat it.' I didn't lose any weight.

When Meisel called me in for a face-to-face meeting, I just dressed as well as I could and tried to keep from looking too nervous. He turned out to be a wonderful guy, shy, good-looking and really polite. He seemed to like me. And he didn't say a word about me being fat.

When I went back to the agency the Ford people were thrilled. Suddenly, I had everyone's attention – my first lesson in the fickle nature of fame.

The shoot itself, at Meisel's studio in New York, was an amazing experience. We were doing a series of Versace dresses, and I was the only model in the story. I was nervous as hell. I walked into the all-white studio and was met by the stylist, a beautiful woman in her mid thirties, who was impeccably stylish. Leading me to a long clothes rail she pulled out a crimson dress and held it up against me. She frowned. Then she pulled a blue top and skirt off the rack and held them up. She smiled, but then her assistant, a mousy young man, frowned. So she re-examined the look and then frowned too. Finally they settled on a simple yellow dress. I loved it, but before I could dress I needed my makeover.

The hair stylist put a long shiny wig on my head. It just didn't feel right, especially after I put on the dress. I'd been told that Steven was very clever so I tried not to worry, thinking that he must know what was right. I stood on a white backdrop with lights shining on me while he sat silently in a chair, staring at me.

'You know what?' he said after a while. 'Take the wig off.'

The stylist took if off. Then Steven picked up his camera and looked at me.

'You're set,' he said.

'What?'

'As soon as they put some gloss on your lips, you're ready. You are perfect.'

The make-up artist came over and did her magic.

'I want you to do whatever you want,' Steven said.

His assistant put some music on.

'Are you serious?' I said, laughing.

'Hell, yeah.'

I suddenly felt free. I started dancing and that's when I saw what a genius he was. He just let me be me. I didn't hold back. We shot picture after picture with me dancing around wearing hoop earrings, short dresses, one sleeved, two sleeved. I had no idea where it all came from, and the pictures were great. That relationship between the model and the photographer can be a fantastic source of energy that just flows through the shoot and can be seen in the pictures.

After that, I flew home to see my mother and catch up with my agent in London. All the other bookers at the agency were suddenly quite respectful of me. It was as if I'd married a prince.

'You did Italian *Vogue*? With Steven? I can't believe you did that so soon.'

I was thinking, You didn't think I could do it, did you?

At about this time Mora decided that she wanted to leave Ford. She didn't have another job so soon she was broke. Now it was my turn to help her: I had saved a lot of money, so I gave her several thousand dollars to tide her over. I've never seen anyone more grateful. Mora was always my champion. She'd given me everything, and watched out for me through it all. I felt I owed it to her.

I was pretty disillusioned with Ford myself. I felt like they never quite understood me, even though I was doing some good projects. It was as if they weren't sure what to do with the Dinka girl.

When Italian *Vogue* came out a few months later, I couldn't believe how Meisel had made me look. He's an incredibly talented photographer and a very generous spirit.

'I haven't seen anybody that interesting, that black and that beautiful in a long time,' he told a reporter.

Steven had shot me wearing Versace, but I didn't meet Gianni Versace himself until several years later, at an after-show party in Paris, when he told me how much he loved my work in the Italian *Vogue* spread. He was such a warm man. Just a few months later I was in a studio in New York when the radio announcer said that Versace had been gunned down outside his lavish home in Miami. I was getting a make-up touch-up after having changed into a new outfit when I heard the news. The make-up artist dropped his brush to the floor. Everyone was very shocked, and we didn't know whether or not he had survived the shooting. We continued with the shoot but everyone had their mind elsewhere.

Even after it was confirmed that he was dead no one could accept the news.

I had seen plenty of death and destruction in my life, but this was different. It made me think again about how crazy people are. It made me realise that life is very fragile – you can be here today and the next minute something terrible happens. He was such a passionate man, but his life was stolen from him.

I'd never been afraid in London or New York, because I associated violence with war. After that I started watching crime shows on television and got really scared if I heard the slightest noise at night. It took me a long time to relax.

It so was great to be in London again. I settled right back into the Sudanese lifestyle, living with my mother and eating dried okra stew. All the things I loved. My mother and her friends were starting to see that my career was real, and it wasn't exploitative. They started to see feel proud of me. I was even invited to the Sudanese community centre to talk to some girls about modelling. There are some younger Sudanese girls working as models.

For a while I commuted from London to New York whenever there was a job. I tried to schedule the editorial jobs, which didn't pay much more than a hundred dollars a day, around advertising work that sometimes paid me eight thousand dollars a day – out of which I had to give the agency their cut. That way the airfare would cover both jobs. It was more economical to fly back and forth than to rent an apartment in New York. I could live at home in London when I wasn't working and stay in hotels, or at Mora's, when I was in New York. Often the companies who hired me would pay my airfare so it worked out well. After a while, as jobs kept coming in, it became apparent that I needed to be in New York full time. The travelling was becoming too much.

I left Ford Models and moved to International Management Group, or IMG. Mora was working there, and I decided to follow her as I felt she understood me more than any other agent I'd met.

I was so busy that I quickly rented an apartment about the size of a minivan on the Lower East Side. I slept on a blanket on the wooden floor for six weeks as I didn't even have time to buy a bed. It felt like being back in the village, in the hut, and I didn't like that at all. I bought a futon at a shop on the corner. They wanted to charge me thirty-five dollars to deliver it so I just picked it up and carried it by myself around the corner and up the stairs, earning cheers from some guys walking by on the street.

'You're a damn strong sister,' one of them said admiringly. After that he called me 'Strong Sister' every time he saw me.

Since my income was so erratic, and I never knew when I would get another job, I tried to save every penny. Really, I saved too much. I've always been a bit of a miser, preferring to have money in the bank for a rainy day than to live an outlandish lifestyle.

I also kept pounding the pavement for work. The thing about being a model is that everyone thinks you can just sit back and be glamorous as the jobs and money roll through the door, but the truth is that you must work hard and treat it seriously like any career. I went on so many go-sees that I can't remember half of them. While I've always loved New York, the city really did feel like the jungle to me. I'd be walking around wondering who was going to leap out from behind a bush and attack me. Which agent was going to eat me. Who was going to ruin my career. It was really stressful. I'd been in the bush, and this, really, wasn't any easier. But that kept me focused.

Over the years I saw many of my fellow models get consumed by partying. When you are a pretty girl in New York, there's always someone who will take you out and give you drugs or liquor in exchange for just being with you. Lots of girls get lost, partying their lives away. It was all too easy. I remember one afternoon I was walking down Broadway when a guy with dreadlocks came up to me, talking fast. He was good-looking and wanted me to come to the party he and his band were holding. He gave me the information and when I got back to the apartment Mora and I looked at it. It turned out that he was one of the guys from the Wu-Tang Clan, one of the biggest rap groups in New York at the time.

I was flattered, but I didn't go. I had too much to do the next morning. I didn't want all my work to be for nothing. I always had my mother in the back of my mind, saying, 'What are you doing wasting all your time? Get to work, girl!' I remembered my father, too. He'd always say, 'Look, Alek, you don't have to be a scientist, or a doctor or a solicitor. But whatever you choose to do, you should really love it. You should focus on it and you must stick with it. Life is not a game, although it can be fun.'

I had a good time and I got good jobs. And, though I didn't know it, I was about to change the face of beauty and modelling in America.

CHAPTER 9

Whether I like it or not, my skin defines me. The first thing many people notice about me is how dark my skin is. Not just in America and Europe but also, to a lesser extent, in the Sudan. In Khartoum my skin marked me as a southerner, probably a Dinka, and many of the lighter-skinned residents of the city looked down on me. Racism exists everywhere.

If I were living in Darfur, where the Sudanese government is committing unspeakable atrocities, my skin would mark me as a *zurqa*, a 'dirty black'. The Arabic militias that are funded and directed by the brutal leaders in Khartoum would single me out, perhaps dropping oil barrels filled with explosives and shrapnel from aeroplanes onto my village, or riding in on a camel to rape, brand and terrorise me. All because I'm black. And they are less black, though darker than most Europeans.

Skin tone is a tricky thing.

I've found that in America many darker-skinned African-Americans both idolise and criticise lighter-skinned

African–Americans. What is this obsession with pigment? Scientists say skin pigment is largely a matter of geography; people who live in sunny areas, such as along the equator, will, over generations, develop darker skin as protection from the sun. People who live in northern areas will develop lighter skin as a more effective way of using the sun's limited rays to manufacture vitamin D. The biology is really quite simple. Unfortunately, the sociology is not.

My skin has both helped me and hurt me in my career. In 1997 the Scottish photographer Albert Watson offered me a job. He has shot every thing from portraits of Keith Richards to dogs looking out from the back of an old station wagon in the Las Vegas desert. When I got to his elaborate studio on Washington Street, in lower Manhattan, I found a gigantic white espresso cup, bigger than a car, resting on its side in the middle of the studio floor. The shoot was for a calendar being published by Lavazza, the Italian coffee company. I was meant to pose on the edge of the cup. My skin was to be the espresso.

Albert was a wonderful man and I immediately felt rapport with him, but when they asked me to take off my clothes I got very nervous. I was uncomfortable with the idea of posing nude. Albert promised me that it would be tasteful, and that I could keep my knickers on. The make-up artist rubbed some sort of oil into my skin to bring out the shine, and the hair stylist put a huge white lily on my head, which made me look like Carmen Miranda. I had to remind myself that this was my first big job – I was earning eight thousand dollars for the shoot, which would be enough to pay my agency the six thousand dollars I owed them for backdated rent and cash advances.

As I walked onto the studio floor it crossed my mind that my mother's fears were being realised: I was posing nude for

161

money. I almost walked off the set. I was so nervous that I couldn't really think so I just sat down in the cup and crossed my legs. My hands were sweating and I struggled not to shake as Albert took the photos.

They are beautiful pictures and I am grateful for the chance I had to work with Albert Watson so early in my career. But as time passes, and I become more aware of race relations in America and Europe, I can't help but compare them to all the images of black people that have been used in marketing over the decades. There was the big-lipped jungle dweller on the Blackamoor ceramic mugs sold in the 1940s; the golliwog badges given away with jam; Little Black Sambo, who decorated the walls of an American restaurant chain in the 1960s; and Uncle Ben, whose apparently benign image still sells rice.

I'm sure no one set out with these exploitative images in mind, but we all carry unconscious inspirations and I think the Lavazza ads reflect the ways in which we typecast people. But hey, I didn't have to do it – I was grateful for the work. After a while, however, I got tired of being seen as just a 'black beauty'.

For instance, in Tina Turner's *GoldenEye* video I appear as a shadowy, mysterious figure, like some apparition from *Heart of Darkness*. For other jobs, the photographers wanted me to pose on leopard print couches straight out of some interior decorator's Tarzan fantasy, or pose with spears. I noticed that journalists often liked to say that I'd been discovered in 'the bush', in Africa. As if I had been a primeval innocent afoot in the forest when the great model agent plucked me from the muck and tamed me, without destroying my savage beauty. I mean, I was wearing jeans in Crystal Palace Park when I was 'discovered'. The closest bush was a well-manicured azalea. I am African, but I am not primitive.

At first, people in the industry never seemed to believe that I could do anything but work that called for 'black' features. That really hurt my feelings. I'd looked around the streets of New York and see that 'all-American' meant frizzy hair, straight hair, dark skin, light skin, big lips, small lips, skinny and curvy – everything under the sun. As far as I'm concerned there are beautiful women all over the world, whether they're Indian, blue-eyed Americans, or green-eyed Mongolian-Swedes. I also knew that most people weren't so limited in their worldview that they'd only respond to images of people who shared their skin colour.

No one ever said to my face that my eyes were too wide set, or that my body was too long or that my hair was too nappy, but on go-sees I'd often be greeted with a bemused expression. The people would mutter under their breath and shake their heads. In my heart I said, 'I'm going to prove all of you wrong. One day you will see that I am not just a model for a certain look. I am no freak, you know!'

That's why it was so great to have Mora in my corner. She really believed in me. When I told her that I no longer wanted to answer any calls from photographers seeking 'black girls' she understood. There's something so disrespectful about that kind of cattle call. I didn't want to go on jobs that discriminated on the basis of skin colour, or that lumped all black girls together. Think about it: which models would spring to mind if some-one asked for all 'white girls'? It would be hard to pick them, right? I wanted to work with people who were creative enough to see beyond that one-dimensional view of the world. Mora agreed. Why bring it all down to black?

★

163

Beauty is such a subjective notion. When I was growing up I never saw myself as beautiful. I looked like my sisters, and like most of the other Dinka girls. We were all dark, tall and lithe. I had the added problem of psoriasis: on the few times I took a look at myself in a mirror, I wasn't pleased.

I am amused these days when people refer to me as having an 'African' look. Africa is not a country; it's a huge continent, filled with many different types of people. Egypt is part of Africa. Madagascar is part of Africa. We're all different. For instance, Ethiopians, in general, would never be mistaken for someone from the Ivory Coast. We have light-skinned Africans and dark-skinned Africans. Short people and tall people. There is no one standard of beauty for Africa.

At last the big designers seem to understand that there's beauty in Africa. They all draw inspiration from Morocco, the Nubian mountains, from all over the continent. The African influence surfaces every couple of years in the collections of Galliano, Ralph Lauren, all of them. They use the inspiration well, so it shouldn't be such a stretch to use models that aren't blonde and pale.

The photographer Gilles Bensimon recognised this, in 1997. At the time, Gilles was the creative director of American *Elle*. The magazine was at the forefront of fashion in those days, and constantly challenged accepted notions of beauty and commerce.

Gilles and I met one day when we were both working in Los Angeles. Neither of us knew that we'd eventually do a picture that would change my life, and the standards by which beauty was judged in America.

He'd heard about me from a go-see I did at *Elle* in New

York. Periodically, I'd visit every major magazine. They'd take Polaroids and put the pictures on their wall. When they came to do a story the editors would get together with the photographers and choose the models that would work best with the clothes. Gilles saw the pictures in New York but called me when he had a shoot scheduled in LA, in an old diner with an elaborate jukebox. Gilles kept putting Elvis records on the jukebox and doing wild dances. I loved it – I thought he was hilarious. Normally I'm quite shy when I first work with someone, but Gilles and I really hit it off.

He told me about his former wife, Elle Mcpherson, who was someone I really admired. He was a really down-to-earth guy in a way, despite his high-flying lifestyle. After that shoot, he kept requesting me for work he was doing. I went to St Barths a couple of times, and out to the Hamptons for shoots on the beach. On one of those beach shoots a stylist almost stepped on a snake and the whole crew freaked out. I just laughed. Snakes didn't really scare me any more. I think Gilles liked that.

He was a painter like me, and we talked often about how satisfying it was to use oils and brushes. Every time I went to his studio I noticed one particular painting that he was working on. I told him that I liked it very much. Years later I went back to the studio and it was still there. He said, 'You always liked this – why don't you take it?' He signed it and now I have his really bright, lovely painting in my home.

We kept working, and my image was constantly in the pages of *Elle*, which was great. But, curiously, it seemed that the other girls he regularly worked with kept getting covers. A cover is a huge deal in the fashion industry. It means you've really arrived, and it gets you lots of work. People who wouldn't normally notice you on the pages of a magazine will see you on the cover. They'll think you have a buzz. If the CEO of a big company likes what he sees he might base a campaign around you. It's very important to get covers. And I'd never had one. Mora and I started to get very frustrated. A year passed. Almost every cover of *Elle* featured a very light-skinned girl. My agent made a call.

'I want to see a cover, Gilles,' she said. 'It's time. She's done so many interior layouts. It isn't fair. It's just because she's African. You guys are too afraid.'

We all knew that the marketing people were afraid to put dark-skinned girls on the covers of fashion magazines. They had research data that they believed showed that people wouldn't buy the magazines unless the cover girl was white or had 'traditional' American features. In 1968, the model Katiti Kironde II was the first black model to appear on the cover of a women's magazine, and there hadn't been many since. *Elle* had run black women, such as Naomi Campbell, a couple of times, but they'd always had more or less 'acceptable' features. None of them looked like me.

We kept nagging Gilles. He had great influence at the magazine but it wasn't his decision. Obviously, he liked the way I looked, because he used me so often for the inside pages, but the management was afraid of losing money by putting me on the cover. Finally, they decided to take a chance.

Gilles called Mora. Everything just fell into place and it was the quickest shoot I'd ever done. He dressed me in just a pure white Armani jacket, open to my navel. He was joking around as usual and I was smiling and laughing.

'Don't stop smiling, but stay still for one second,' he said.

I stopped.

He took the shot.

And that's the one that ran on my very first cover. I was quite proud of how I looked. In the photograph I'm standing at an angle, so you can see my chest beneath the open jacket. Not that it reveals anything but skin. I'm looking right at the camera with a half smile on my face. It was elegant and fresh at the same time. Gilles made no attempt to hide my natural features – my full lips, my skin, my tightly curled hair. It was a magnificent picture, printed on an all-white background, with gold type.

The issue sold like crazy and it seemed that every newspaper and magazine in America wrote about how the cover challenged our traditional conceptions of beauty. The *New York Times* interviewed Gilles.

'The statement is, "Nobody is out, everybody is in",' he said.

The reader response was overwhelming. Thousands of women, and more than a few men, wrote in to praise the cover. They were Chinese, American Indian, African-American, Caucasian, Indian, Brazilian, Guatemalan, French, English and Icelandic people. Almost all of them said they found the cover shot liberating.

'Hey – thanks for putting *me* on the cover. Finally I have someone I can identify with,' wrote one girl.

'Cool,' wrote another. 'I'm a white teenaged boy but I felt like having Alek Wek on your cover means that the world is becoming a bigger place – keep it up!'

Oprah Winfrey even invited me on her show. That was one of the high points of my life, because she is such an intelligent, gracious woman. She talked about what it had been like for her to grow up in a culture that didn't value blackness, and that encouraged everyone, no matter what their natural attributes were, to conform to the image of white American beauty. 'This is a new day, America!' she proclaimed to the television audience. 'When I was growing up, if you'd been on the cover of a magazine, I would have had a whole different concept of who I was.'

That cover raised me to a level of fame that I never could have imagined. It felt like such a positive thing: I really had a strong voice now. Suddenly I symbolised a kind of freedom from fashion tyranny for a lot of people. I remember that I was walking along 14th Street in New York one afternoon when a nurse ran up to me and said, 'Normally I don't like models but you are just amazing. You are real.'

Near my house girls would stop me and give me a hug. Total strangers. There were stories in all the magazines, and reports on TV. Even people who didn't care about fashion were talking about that cover. I was so surprised. At times I felt like a bit of a freak.

Doors began to open wider after that, but I still faced a kind of institutional racism within the fashion industry. It wasn't that most of the people were actual racists – they didn't go to KKK meetings or anything like that. Rather, it was that they followed a set of assumptions that had been passed down to them. For instance, during my second season on the catwalk I wanted to work with Karl Lagerfeld, but the people in Paris said I wasn't right for him, meaning, of course, that I was too 'exotic'. They felt that Chanel was not about being exotic – or dark skinned.

I finagled a go-see and he said that I was perfect. Karl is a creative genius and he never stops working or thinking. He's definitely not someone to get stuck in the past. He told me that he felt my features and my look represented the future of fashion. He put me on the catwalk, for Chanel. I did a lot of work for him, and later, when I started my handbag business, he gave me advice.

A few years ago Karl asked me to work at the Chanel shows in Paris. It was such an honour just to be there, and so I was completely blown away when he fitted me for the wedding dress that traditionally closes each fashion show.

'The standards of beauty changed, and she is the expression of modernity in beauty,' Lagerfeld told a TV reporter who had come to his atelier in Paris. 'It's important to have her, because the world is not just basic blonde.'

A similar thing happened with John Galliano, the wildly creative British designer. I worked with him several time, and we got along well. After I'd been in the business about four years, he took the helm at Dior. I'd never done anything with Dior and I thought it would be a great opportunity.

I kept telling my Paris agent to try to get me a booking. Again, people thought I wouldn't be right. I couldn't understand it. I thought they could at least see me wearing his designs before they wrote me off. So we badgered them until, finally, they said, 'You know what? Great. Send her over for a look.'

I arrived to find them deeply involved with lace. Everything was white and pink and baby blue lace, along with hats from the 1930s and cameo brooches. They had me try on an outfit with a baby blue veil covered with sequins, along with a hat and lots of jewellery. I walked out to where John and the others were, and they said, 'Walk up and down.'

As I moved, I felt it. I knew I looked great. It's just a sensation I get once in a while.

I could see their eyes. They were looking at each other. I

was hoping they'd book me. Then Galliano smiled and I almost swooned.

They didn't say a word. Just took a Polaroid of me and sent me on my way.

My phone rang as I was heading for the Métro.

'He loved you!' said Mora.

The *Elle* cover helped a very great deal, but it didn't make being a black model a rosy experience. Still, my career progressed rapidly after we broke that cover colour barrier. And why not? It's a business, really. People started to see that money had no colour. My image could sell as well as any of the other top models. In time, I would be named 'Model of the Decade' by *i-D* magazine; one of *People* magazine's 'Fifty Most Beautiful People,' and one of the 'Fifty Most Influential Faces in Fashion' by both *i-D* and *Frank* magazines.

I don't like to complain. I've done really well in my life, but I can describe what it's like to be a black woman in the modern world. In the Sudan I didn't notice race that much, until I got to Khartoum. When I moved to England, the children at school called me 'Midnight Black' and most of the white people would either ignore me completely or treat me as some exotic specimen to be feared or pitied.

In New York I get such a variety of reactions that it's hard to predict what will happen on any given day. Lots of people – men and women, young and old, of all races – recognise me and say positive things to me. There are a number of African men who sell things on the street, like counterfeit watches and handbags. When I walk along Canal Street they'll call out to me in languages I don't understand. They think I'm one of them, but I'm Dinka, from the Sudan. In Paris, an African guy ran up to me and said, 'You're from Perl. You're from Perl.' And I said, 'No, I'm not.' He was convinced, just based on my looks, yet he was totally wrong. I didn't even know where he was talking about.

The strangest things happen. In a train station once a woman came up to me and insisted that I was Waris Dirie, the Somalian model who wrote a book called *Desert Flower*. I said I was flattered, because she's beautiful and wrote a wonderful book, but that I wasn't her. People constantly confuse me with Naomi Campbell. That, to me, is ridiculous – we don't look a thing alike.

Not long ago I was walking up a street in Fort Greene, Brooklyn, not far from my house, with my boyfriend Riccardo Sala. He's Italian, light-skinned and about six feet tall. He's a really nice guy, and he's used to people staring at us as though we were the odd couple when we walk down the street. That day we were heading off to brunch, holding hands, when a car full of men with dreadlocks slowed down as they passed.

'Traitor! Sell out!' one of them shouted at me in a deep West Indian accent.

He didn't like to see the African model holding hands with a white guy, apparently.

Riccardo was fine about it. He understands. We just walked on, keeping our heads high.

Sometimes the stereotyping becomes more serious, and disrespectful to the point of making me really angry. Once I landed at JFK after doing several jobs in Europe. I travel with a British passport, but I've got a 'green card', which allows me to live and work in America with most of the rights of a nat-uralised citizen. I pay a lot of taxes; I own a house; and I run my handbag business here. There's no question that I'm legitimate.

When I reached the immigration booth the officer of Homeland Security looked me up and down and studied my passport with extra care.

I thought, not again. I have learned not to say anything in this situation. There's nothing you can say to help yourself, and plenty you can do that will irritate the officials. I've been detained so many times. I've come to realise that as a successful black woman – and a tall one at that – I represent something that triggers hostility and suspicion on a lot of people, black and white, male and female. It still surprises me that it happens in America and Europe, where people are supposed to be well educated and sophisticated.

Anyway, the immigration official sent me off to the little room they have for suspected terrorists, border jumpers and the like. I've been there before. They took my picture. They checked my green card again. They double-checked my fingerprints. They acted really tough, cold and suspicious. They kept me for two and a half hours. I'd just flown business class from Frankfurt. I was wearing nice clothes, carrying a bag that I'd designed, which even had a little brass tag with my name on it. I had all my papers. Yet still they had to detain me for all that time. Was it because I'm a black woman? I can't prove it, but experience tells me that my skin figured in there somewhere.

A few weeks later I was on my way to another job. I had to fly to Munich, then Frankfurt and then back to New York, all in the space of six days. I was tired, so I ducked into the business class lounge at JFK, looking forward to having a cup of tea in peace while I waited for my flight. The man at the desk looked me over as I handed him my boarding pass. He swiped it through his machine and said, 'Have a seat.'

I put my bag down and made a cup of tea. As I took my first sip a voice came over the loudspeaker:

'Miss Alek Wek, would you please come to the desk.'

I looked in my bag to make sure I hadn't left my boarding pass at the desk. It was there. So I walked up to the desk.

'You called me?'

He didn't look up from his computer. I stood there for a moment. Finally he looked up, with a condescending face.

'I've been examining your information,' he said.

'Yes?'

'Let me see your boarding pass again.'

I handed it to him.

'Are you certain that you purchased or upgraded to a business class ticket?'

'You saw it. I checked in with it.'

'I'm not certain that you are allowed in the business class lounge,' he said, looking me over. I could tell it wasn't my ticket he was worried about. It was me.

'What are you saying?'

'I'm saying that I'm not certain that I can allow you to stay in the lounge.'

For a moment, I was speechless.

'Where are you from?' he asked.

'What does that have to do with anything? I have a business class ticket and I want to have a cup of tea and then I'll get out of here and you can go about your business however you want. But for now, just leave me alone.'

I was furious. I walked back to my seat so I wouldn't start shouting at him. I always travel with the same airlines. I use the same travel agent. This guy was looking for a problem. He was trying to find a way to devalue me, to make me small. I didn't like that one bit. It was degrading and I don't think he would have tried to pull that on a man, especially a white man.

I sat there for a few minutes. I was livid. Suddenly the guy appeared and handed me my boarding pass.

'It's OK,' he said.

'No, it's not OK,' I said.

'What?'

'You do not have a right to question me like that. You imply that I don't deserve a good seat. That maybe I can't afford to pay for it. That I might not be good enough to fly business class to Europe. Why is that? Why have you chosen me out of all these people? Because I'm an African woman?'

He was silent. Then he walked away. I finally got to finish my tea. As I waited, the man's shift must have ended because he wasn't at the door when I left the business class lounge. Instead, there was a young African-American woman with long, beautiful hair.

'Alek Wek!' she said excitedly when she saw me. 'How are you?'

I'd seen her many times before while waiting for flights. She was a lovely girl. I had a pleasant flight after that.

Believe it or not, when I came back from that marathon trip the Department of Homeland Security detained me once again. I was tired. I felt insulted. I didn't understand what was going on. I had just been through this a few weeks before. It was the same guy who'd questioned me the last time. This time he grilled me about my travels. Why was I in Africa? He looked at each page of my passport. Why had I been to Egypt the year before? Why this? Why that?

'I'm a model. I travel for work,' I said.

He looked me up and down like he didn't believe me. I wondered if Cindy Crawford had these kinds of issues.

'Why are you interrogating me?'

'It's for your own protection, you know.'

'I don't feel very safe.'

It's like a jail in there. You can't use your phone to call for assistance. They won't tell you why you're being detained. Another hour passed. I went up to him and told him that I knew my rights.

'Your rights?' he said with a smirk.

Finally, after two and a half hours, he stamped my passport.

'I thought you were Naomi Campbell,' one of the other officials said.

I just shook my head and walked out. I couldn't bring myself to say thank you.

While I was waiting for my luggage a woman came up to me and said, 'You know, you look just like this model. She's from Africa. She's got really short hair and she looks just like you.'

'Really?' I said.

'Really,' she said. 'It's amazing.'

I was too tired to talk to her. But I appreciated her interest.

I got in the car and put all the bad exchanges I'd had during this trip behind me. I didn't want to revisit those negative thoughts. I try never to take the same road twice. It's the Dinka way. If you follow the same path you'll end up in the same place, or worse. I let others deal with their issues and move ahead. I've got a life to live.

CHAPTER 10

Mora called one crisp Saturday morning and we started talking about apartments. Real estate is an obsession shared by all New Yorkers, since good apartments are so hard to find. It was early winter and I was paying over a thousand dollars a month for a ten foot by fourteen foot dump on the Lower East Side. The landlord had slapped up a tissue-thin wall across a studio, called it a one-bedroom apartment and hiked up the rent. The kitchen had a chipped sink and a three-burner stove. The building was so flimsy I could hear my neighbours clear their throats. It felt like I was just pouring money down the drain.

'Come out to Brooklyn and have a look,' Mora said. 'The places are great out here and a lot cheaper.'

The idea excited me. I'd always liked her neighbourhood. I was earning more money than I'd ever seen and maybe I could find a great place out there. On the spur of the moment I caught the A train out to Clinton Hill, a place that at the time, in 1997, was just in the initial stages of a gentrification process that would end up making it, and neighbouring Fort Greene, one of the coolest places in Brooklyn. Of course, back then we had no way of knowing what would happen to Brooklyn real estate prices in the coming years. In those days most Manhattanites still saw the borough as a rough, distant place, not the desirable centre of cool it has become.

Mora and I shared a love of driving around the city, listening to music and checking out places we'd never before seen. It promised to be a pretty great day, even if we didn't find a house. We piled into her jeep and drove down to a junction in Fort Greene where realtors posted listings in their windows. For some reason my eyes were drawn to just one category: Buildings for Sale.

'That one looks nice,' said Mora, pointing to a three-storey red brick townhouse that was listed at 395,000 dollars.

'Are you kidding? You know I don't have anywhere near that much money in the bank.'

'You borrow it, Alek. You get a mortgage.'

'No way!' In Dinka culture it's almost unheard of to borrow money. My mother had always stressed that a person should never buy anything they can't afford or pay for outright. This idea of getting a mortgage was so foreign to me that I couldn't even begin to understand it: you borrow a hundred thousand dollars and end up paying the bank two hundred thousand dollars over the life of the loan? That seemed ridiculous.

'Let's just a get a list of houses and we'll go see some of them,' Mora said. 'There's no harm in looking.'

'OK. But I'm not buying anything I can't afford.'

We drove around and looked at about ten houses that morning. We got a lot of laughs because most of the houses were terrible. We couldn't imagine how people lived in them.

One house stank so badly from the ten cats the owner kept I couldn't go into some of the rooms. Another one was leaning so far to the left I thought it might fall over. One was so dodgy looking, with windows right at street level, I was afraid a robber would break in as soon as the moving van pulled away from the kerb.

All the time I was wondering how I could possibly pay for a house. Mora made it sound really simple, if daunting. If I put 10 per cent down I could pay the rest off monthly until I was over fifty years old. It sounded crazy, but I realised that it wasn't as crazy as paying rent.

As we pulled up to the last house of the day I realised it was the red brick one I'd admired in the real estate office window. For some reason, it made me think of my childhood home in Wau, even though they didn't look at all alike. There was a feeling, an energy about the place that spoke to my heart. The house said, 'Home'.

As we walked to the entrance the real estate broker said, 'Now be aware that this is a very little house. Most of the others on this block are huge. I don't want you to be disappointed.'

We entered on the ground floor and my eyes opened wide. Nice, I thought.

'Look, it's completely renovated,' Mora whispered to me.

'Wouldn't it be brilliant to own a house?' I said.

I could feel my fears giving way to desire.

We went upstairs and when I saw the living room with its high ceiling, beautiful fireplace and the sun pouring in through the floor-to-ceiling windows I said, 'Oh my God!' out loud. The realtor smiled. She could see how much I loved it.

'Let's go to the top floor,' she said.

I gave Mora a puzzled look.

'You didn't know there was another floor?'

I couldn't believe it. I thought we'd already seen the whole thing. Mora took me aside and said, 'Alek, you've got to live in this house. It's, like, totally you.'

'Too bad I can't afford it,' I said. 'It's nearly four hundred thousand dollars!'

'So? You're working so hard. You should own your own house.'

The realtor told us someone else was about to make an offer, and that the house was going to go quickly.

In the jeep Mora said, 'You are going to get this house.'

It was right before Christmas and I'd planned to go to London to see my mother.

'Cancel that trip,' instructed Mora.

So I did. Mora walked me through the process of buying the house. We got a surveyor to check it out, and then I got my accountant and business adviser, who lived in Cleveland, to start on the paperwork. I learned about mortgages as we went along. Fortunately, I trusted him.

He was shocked at the price.

'In Cleveland you'd have a swimming pool and a four-car garage for that price,' he said.

'Well this is New York, not Ohio. I'm sure that if we went to Timbuktu we'd get a whole city block for that kind of money. I don't want to live in either of those places.'

He wouldn't let me bid on it until he saw it. He was such a nice guy that he flew all the way out from Ohio to have a look. He climbed the ladder up to the roof, looked around and said, 'This is too much responsibility for you.'

I told him that I was already paying twelve hundred dollars

a month in rent, plus utilities and everything else for a tiny apartment in Manhattan.

'You really want it, don't you?'

'Yes. I'm not going to give up.'

I even surprised myself by how much I wanted that house.

'Okay then, let me get to work on it.' Once he saw the appraisal, he realised I was getting a fair deal.

In the end, the other potential buyer went away for Christmas. I stayed in New York, put my 10 per cent deposit down and got the house. Suddenly, I had a mortgage that was costing me more than my rent. Later I was able to refinance it and get it down to a fifteen-year mortgage. Wow, I thought, when I'm forty, I'll own this place outright. All of a sudden I was an upstanding member of the community with a mortgage to pay and pipes to fix.

I bought furniture, but not very much. Then when I was doing a shoot for Coach, the leather goods company, I suggested they pay me in furniture. They gave me two incredibly beautiful leather couches for my living room. The house gave me a lot of impetus to work on my career. I started to realise that if you need money you will make it. Your needs will be met. I also devoted more time to my painting as I had enough space to set a whole room aside as a studio.

Once again, my life was changing rapidly. It quickly became clear that since Brooklyn was such a vast place I'd need to learn how to drive as well. I'd ridden in cars only a few times when I lived in the Sudan. I'd never driven one. I signed up for lessons with a firm that had cars with two steering wheels and two sets of brakes. I found it very hard, but fun too. I must have scared the instructor half to death, but I learned in the end. Once I passed my test I got my own jeep and became the first person in my family ever to own a car.

When my mother came for a visit and saw my house and my car she said, 'Welcome to America, Alek.' She couldn't believe it. We'd always dreamed about owning a home. And here it was. It was very humbling. I'd attained what so many immigrants hoped for when they come to America. I keep a portrait I painted of my father on the wall in my home. It's black and white and grey, about four feet tall. Whenever I look at that painting I feel grounded, at home.

Despite all this, something was missing from my life. I'd seen stories about the Sudan on television, especially a spate of reports about the 'Lost Boys', and my heart ached for my home country. The Lost Boys of Sudan was a programme run by the International Rescue Committee to resettle boys from the Sudan who'd lost their homes and families in the war. The boys had gathered in large groups and escaped into the bush to avoid the government-supported militias that were bearing down on all the villages in the southern Sudan.

Some of them made epic journeys across the country into Ethiopia and Kenya, usually with no money and little food – one boy walked naked for hundreds of miles because he couldn't find any clothes. There were more boys than girls, because the girls were more frequently kidnapped or killed with their families.

About four thousand of these boys were eventually resettled in America. I really felt for these children and as I was getting so much publicity I thought I might be able to raise awareness of Sudan's plight in this country and Europe. Many fashion magazines and newspapers were beginning to write about me.

I realised that I was very lucky to have a public voice, and I didn't want to waste it. I knew I couldn't just sit in my nice house, enjoying the fruits of my hard work and very good luck. I also felt guilty: why was I alive and doing so well when so many of my countrymen were suffering?

The situation in my country was absolutely atrocious. Government soldiers and militias were burning down entire Dinka villages, sometimes with the women and children forced to remain in their huts and burn to death. The killers would charge on camels into groups of tribesmen and hack their limbs off. It was terrifying. I felt hopeless, and vulnerable, having been a refugee myself, despite all my success. Once you've been attacked by soldiers and forced from your home you never quite feel that the world is a safe place, no matter where you end up. I had seen so much death and destruction that I could never believe that tomorrow was guaranteed.

I didn't want to live a life where everything revolved around me. That wasn't my style, but I wasn't sure how I could exploit the attention I was getting to focus attention on the Sudan. My friends were always fascinated when I talked about what was going on in there:

'You mean people are starving there?'

'Yes. And they are being murdered. Their homes burned.'

'Why don't I ever see anything about this in the papers?'

I thought this was a very good question. I decided to change that.

Every time anyone interviewed me I'd start telling my story, and talk about the Sudan. The journalists would usually want to know about the catwalk, the shoots, the glamour. I'd give them a bit of that, to keep their interest, but then I'd submerge them in talk about Africa. They started printing it. An article

182

in the *New York Times* caught a lot of people's attention, including someone at the US Committee for Refugees and Immigrants (USCRI).

They wrote me a letter asking for my assistance. They were offering hope. They too believed in the possibilities for the future. It was heaven-sent.

'These people are incredible,' Mora told me when she read the letter.

I met with the group, and they asked me to be a spokesperson. They even said that we might go to the Sudan together. I began by telling my story at schools in the New York area. The children were always mesmerised by what I said and asked a lot of questions. They rarely seemed to understand why something so terrible had happened. That made me realise that I didn't really understand it either.

I was sure that we could make things better. I remembered when I was a child, and UNICEF came to Wau to build the well pumps that provided clean water for the whole town. It made such a difference to our lives. More wells were needed, all over the Sudan, and especially in the rural areas, where people still sometimes have to walk for two hours to collect drinking water.

Mora and I went to Washington, DC to meet with the president of USCRI, a man called Roger Winter. I was very nervous. My background hadn't given me much preparation for dealing with important people and I wasn't sure that it was going to go well at all. He turned out to be wonderful. He was passionate about the Sudan, and knew far more than I did about the situation in my own country. I just loved him.

When he offered to take me to the Sudan, so that publicity would raise worldwide awareness of the situation, I told him I couldn't. I had surrendered my Sudanese passport to the British and I thought this might anger the Sudanese government. I was afraid that if they caught me they might not ever let me leave, given that I was a high-profile refugee.

I broke down and wept in his office when he started talking about going back to the Sudan, because it brought back such a flood of memories. It had been nearly ten years since I left Khartoum and the idea of travelling there frightened me. Mora wept with me, concerned for my feelings, but the more I thought about it, the more I realised that I needed to face my country again, to deal with my fear.

The situation there was terrible. President al-Bashir had recently clamped down even harder on non-Muslims, and soon after he declared that women were no longer allowed to work in public. President Clinton had recently ordered the bombing of a pharmaceutical factory that the Americans believed was connected with terrorists. I couldn't help but think what would have happened to me if I'd stayed in my country: rape, murder, enslavement. I wanted to scream, but I realised that the best way to scream would be to do it so others could hear, all around the world. I could accomplish a lot by going back and generating publicity for USCRI.

Roger Winter told me to take some time to think about it. Then, while Mora and I were still in Washington, we went on a private tour of the White House. We didn't meet President Clinton but we got an insider's view of that incredible place. Another day a congressman invited me to discuss flights to and from Africa, and I met Hillary Clinton at that meeting. She struck me as a really strong woman and I admire her very much. I thought of all the difficult things she had faced. I decided to say yes to the trip to the Sudan. The

USCRI officials said that, unfortunately, the trip wouldn't include visits to any areas where my family were living. Also, since it was illegal for me to return, we'd have to go through Kenya, with the permission of the SPLA soldiers who controlled that border.

On the flight back to New York I thought about the Sudan, and how far from home I was. There isn't much of a Sudanese community in New York so I hardly ever saw my countrymen. I missed them. In London my family had a great group of Sudanese friends. On my last trip home my mother had gathered a group of women together and we'd celebrated with songs and conversation. They knew I was a success now, but they didn't treat me any differently. They were happy and proud, of course, but they didn't make a fuss. The older ones were still living pretty traditional lives, even in London. For my mother, the community served as an anchor in her life. She had friends who grew up the same way as her and understood all that she had been through. They didn't talk about walking through the forest with their children to escape murderers, or what it was like to watch your husband die from lack of medical care. Rather, they shared their tips for how best to dry okra on tin pans above the stove instead of in the tropical sun. They got together and cooked stews and *kissra*. It was very important for them to have those connections.

I'd also been really pleased to see all the people I used to hang out with. I still felt very much a part of that community. Psychologically, it was so important for me to connect with my fellow Dinka, even though people my age were doing all kinds of things as they adjusted to the new world. For instance, one of my many cousins came from a village to London and ended up going to college and meeting a man from Ireland. They married and had a beautiful Irish-Dinka baby. At first the older Dinka women, of my mother's generation, gossiped about her as she had married outside her culture, but eventually they accepted her, and now her baby is considered a true Dinka too.

One night I went to see some young Sudanese musicians who were making music in a London recording studio. A girl was singing, while a man ran some beats through the board. It was great. She was over six feet tall and gorgeous, in a Diane von Furstenberg wrap dress and red shoes. I felt like a little shrimp next to her. She'd just had a successful meeting with a record executive and had bought a bottle of champagne to celebrate. I realised how far we were from where we all grew up. Then a guy from Zimbabwe walked in. He'd just finished a recording. He'd been a boy soldier back in Africa, and he showed us where he'd been shot. It was crazy. We were all living in the modern world, but we had all experienced the violence of the old world, in Africa. Early the next morning I flew to New York. After the plane landed I headed straight to my house to take it easy until the morning, when I had a shoot. Mora called to tell me that she had decided that she wanted to go with me to the Sudan, and that USCRI and World Vision International would team up to send us. I called my mother and told her the good news.

'Alek, you stay at home,' she ordered me.
'But Mother,' I pleaded. 'I have to go.'
'It's too dangerous. They'll kill you and Mora.'
'We'll be safe. It's important.'
Finally she relented.

'Try to see my sister if you can,' my mother said.

I didn't have the heart to tell her that USCRI had said that wouldn't be part of the agenda.

My twenty-first birthday was coming up and people were getting excited about it. I'd never celebrated my birthday in the Sudan, first, because I didn't really know the actual date of my birth, and second, because we just didn't celebrate birthdays back home. In England we'd adapted to the culture by serving little cakes on birthdays, but nothing extravagant. In New York I'd been to a few big birthday parties and had always been a bit puzzled by all the champagne and celebration. People, including Mora, were pushing me to celebrate too. I decided to host a birthday fund-raiser for USCRI.

The club impresario Amy Sacco offered us her new venue, Lot 61, and Mora persuaded a DJ from Hot 97 to donate his time and equipment. My model friends, such as Carolyn Murphy and Bridget Hall, came but, best of all, my sister flew in from Canada and my seven-foot-tall cousin, who just astonished everyone, drove up from Washington, DC. There were USCRI people there, along with people from various other charitable organisations, so it was a real mix of people: fashion, media and relief work. We projected pictures of the Sudan onto the walls and we danced late into the night. Everyone had to pay twenty dollars to get in, as a donation. We raised over six thousand dollars that night.

Not long after that the USCRI people told us we had to get some vaccinations before going on the trip.

'But I'm from the Sudan,' I said. 'I don't need any jabs. I've already been exposed to everything.'

'Talk to the doctor,' they said.

Mora and I visited a tropical medicine clinic in New York and the doctor literally scared the pants off us. He told me that I'd been gone so long I needed to be protected. Any natural immunity would probably have faded. Mora definitely needed protection. They told us about all the horrible diseases in the area we were going to visit. There's mycetoma, a chronic inflammatory disease that ruins your skin; schistosomiasis, an infectious disease that causes swelling of the liver and spleen; tuberculosis, one of the main health problems in the country; leishmaniases, a parasitic disease passed by flies; leprosy; malaria — well, I knew all about that — and . . . Mora's eyes were on stalks.

'Give me whatever you think I need,' she said.

The doctor looked at me.

'I'll go along with that,' I said.

Our arms were swollen from all the vaccinations, and we had to take our trousers off so they could stick huge needles into our thigh muscles to deliver gammaglobulin, which helps prevent hepatitis. We had to return to the clinic two more times. It was crazy. I'd hardly ever had an injection in my life, and now I was full of holes.

Finally, we were ready to go.

'What should I pack?' Mora asked.

'It's going to be hot,' is all I said. 'And it's not going to be fancy.'

Mora, Roger Winter and I went out to the airport after work one day to head for Africa. By this time, I was used to flying business class, or even first class on long flights. It's amazing how quickly I had become spoilt, and I have to admit that I loved the pampering. For this trip, however, we didn't want to waste USCRI's money so we flew economy class. We were bound for Nairobi, with several stops at airports along the way.

After a stopover in Nairobi we caught a small propeller plane to Lokichokio, near the border of the Sudan. From there, we drove in Land Rovers to a smaller airport where we were to catch a flight over the border. The plane had to fly at a high altitude in case the Sudanese military decided to shoot it down, but soon we found ourselves descending into a dirt landing strip in a town called Marial.

As we got close to the ground a group of children started running towards the plane. I was afraid we'd run them over. When we got out onto the landing strip the children yelled at me and Mora.

'*Awai, awai, awai!*'

'What are they saying?' Mora asked me.

'Salt. They're saying, "Salt, salt, salt!" Salt is like gold around here.'

Then they started laughing, saying '*kawaje*' and pointing at Mora.

'That means "white",' I told her.

They looked at me in my Timberland boots and my jeans, my bright blue vest and Louis Vuitton headscarf, and their jaws dropped open.

'I can't believe she's a Dinka,' one girl said.

'That's right, I'm Dinka,' I said, 'but not her,' I continued, pointing to Mora. 'She's American.'

We smiled to mask how painful it was to see these children, who looked desperate, frightened, confused by the war.

'We have to hurry along, Alek,' said leader of the trip. 'We've had a change of plan. Our original route is too dangerous so now we're going to El Tonj.'

'El Tonj? But that's where my mother's family is from!'

I was so excited. Maybe I'd get to see my aunt.

'Radio ahead if you can,' I said. 'Tell them we're coming.'

The journey out to El Tonj was a very curious affair, because we were heading through territory controlled by SPLA rebels rather than the Sudanese government. Rebel groups are usually portrayed as being vicious thugs outside the rule of law, but these men, in their simple uniforms, were more polite than many immigration officials I've encountered at airports around the world. They even filled out travel papers for us so we wouldn't be detained by SPLA members inside the country. They understood that our goal was to help the powerless people within the country. We weren't really interested in the politics of the war.

Our first day out, we got so stuck in the mud that we all had to get out and push the Land Rovers to firmer ground.

'Can't they call a tow truck?' Mora asked.

I knew she was kidding, but it was true that we were out in the middle of nowhere, with no one to help us.

Mora was a tough girl, who hiked a lot and enjoyed camping. Once she even invited me to bungee jump off the Brooklyn Bridge with her and some friends.

'No way. I left the Sudan to save my skin – I'm not about to risk my life with a bunch of lunatics in New York!'

'Chicken!' she teased me.

Southern Sudan, however, showed her she wasn't quite as tough as she thought. Africa was a more than she'd expected, and she freaked out. On our first night we slept in a dirt-floored concrete hut used by relief workers. They'd dug holes out under each hut that they could dive into if planes started bombing the camp. As Mora was falling asleep a lizard fell onto her sleeping bag and she screamed blue murder. The bugs terrified her too.

'Oh my God!' she said every time she saw something strange.

I just laughed. Welcome to my world.

The next day we drove across an endless stretch of parched earth, brown and cracked from the sun. Our heads banged against the windows as the Land Rover rumbled over the ruts and bounced off rocks. Then we entered the forest, where we drove more slowly because the road was curvy and wet. Finally we reached El Tonj, where a lot of international relief workers had set up operations. An hour or so after that we reached a small village.

'This is it?' asked Mora, looking around at the collection of huts and stone buildings, and the large cattle camp.

'I lived in a place like this for six months when I was a girl,' I said.

This village, which usually had about six hundred people, was different from the one my family had stayed in. There were thousands of refugees living in the stone buildings, under tables in the market – which had nothing much for sale besides cigarettes and soap – and in flimsy tents. A tall, thin man wearing a turquoise boiler suit stood nearby, chewing on a stick. A few women in long muu-muus and headscarves sat on a bench. The air was thick with smoke from the cooking fires, a smell that took me back to my childhood. My emotions were thick in my body and I felt like sitting down and clutching my knees. I missed my mother for a moment.

We weren't there for more than half an hour before I saw an old woman approaching on the path. She looked frantic. As she got closer, I realised it was my mother's younger sister, Alwet. She was older now, but I still recognised her. She used to come from the village for weeks at a time and take care of me. She still stood tall, though her hair had streaks of grey. 'Auntie Alwet!' I cried out in Dinka.

It was so lovely to see her.

We held each other and cried deep sobs. She had thought she'd never see us again. I felt so much emotion; I'd never expected it to be this deep. This was the aunt we all loved so much, who had suffered so badly. Not just from the war, which, judging by how thin and wizened she looked, had caused her a lot of hardship, but also before the war.

When I was young Alwet married a rough man. After two years they still hadn't been able to have children. Of course the man blamed her – a Dinka village man would never even imagine that infertility might be his own fault. In his frustration he beat her, demanding that she give him a child. Then he decided she was useless, returning her to her father and demanding the cows back that he had given in marriage payment. That was a great humiliation for her and the family. Alwet accepted her husband's rejection, left the marriage and started living by herself and raising her own crops. She was an outcast in the village but through it all she retained a quiet dignity. Years later I helped her get to Kenya, to escape the oppression she faced in the village. She adopted two children that had been orphaned and emigrated to Australia, where, slowly, she learned to adjust to modern life.

That day she said that when she heard through the bush telegraph that one of my mother's daughters was on the way she gathered some of my other relatives, whom I didn't know, and walked for hours. She didn't know which girl she was going to find – me, or one of my four sisters. She looked so thin, so tired and so worn out that I began sobbing. She put her arms around me and said, 'Don't cry Alek. Why are you crying? Life is good.'

We stood in a circle, catching up on all the news. Mora stood to the side, unable to understand a word.

Then I told Mora that my relatives wanted to sacrifice a goat in order to bless us and unite us once again with the ancestral spirits.

'You're kidding, right?' she said.

I told her that animal sacrifice is central to Dinka rituals. We rarely slaughter animals just for food, but on important occasions we will kill them to please the spirits that surround us. Mora couldn't bear the thought of watching them kill the goat that they'd brought with them. She begged me not to let them do it.

'Look at that animal,' she said, pointing to the dusty, long-haired goat. 'We can't have them kill it just for us.'

'Mora,' I said, 'this is what we do.'

'I can't watch.'

'I'll ask them to use a chicken instead. Will that be all right?' She bit her lip and nodded her head. My relatives agreed. We'd only been standing there talking for about fifteen minutes when a woman appeared out of the bush, leading one child by the hand and holding a baby in her other arm. The woman had a terrified look on her face. Her clothes were rags. The child had sticks for legs, forehead and eyes jutted forward unnaturally and his belly was swollen with thick veins coming up through the skin. The baby in her arms was almost unconscious, her eyes rolling back into her head. She was dying.

Help me,' the mother wailed.

Flies nipped at the baby.

'My baby,' she said.

The baby looked nearly dead from malnutrition. A yellow crust surrounded its eyes. It was listless, rotting in soiled clothes. I'd never seen anything so awful.

'We haven't had any food in weeks,' she said and fell to the ground.

'We've got to get this baby to a feeding station,' I said.

Relief groups ran centres in the area to help starving people, but you had to get to their tents before you could find help. I wanted to stay with my family but I couldn't bear to see this child die.

My family, however, had other ideas. They'd seen this kind of child over and over. To them it was a fact of life.

'It's just what we live with every day,' my aunt said. 'It's so frightening but there's nothing we can do about it. We must proceed with the sacrifice, or else the spirits won't be appeased.'

When I told Mora what my aunt said, a horrified look crossed her face.

'We must,' my aunt said. 'Or the spirits will be angry.'

'OK,' I said, asking the starving woman from the bush to sit under a tree with her children. We gave her a tin cup of water while one of the men who had come with my aunt took a chicken in his arms and recited some incantations, invoking the ancestors. Then he sliced the chicken's neck with a knife so the blood spurted out. It was so awful. This woman was about to die, and here we were doing a ritual that really didn't mean that much to me, since I'd grown up so far from it. I'll never forget that scene. I kept glancing at the child and saying to myself, 'Please God, don't let her die.'

My family didn't want to see her die, either. They rushed through the sacrifice. One of the men held the chicken by its

194

legs and cut off its head with a spear. They set the body on the ground and it started running around headless as the elders chanted prayers to reintroduce me to the spirit world, which I'd left behind when I moved to London, and to protect Mora and me on our journey. Then one of the men dipped the chicken in some water and, holding it by its legs, whirled it around to spray water and blood everywhere.

A few minutes later I picked up the baby and we drove her to the feeding station an hour away. To call it that makes it sound almost like a place you'd fatten livestock. Sadly, it was far worse than that.

The place was run by Médecins Sans Frontières, or Doctors Without Borders. They immediately took in the family and put special bands on the children's arms, round their biceps. The bands, called 'bracelets of life', were marked with bright gradations of green, yellow, red and orange. When the doctor pulled the bracelet tight the colour that was left would tell them how seriously malnourished the child was. These two were red, meaning that, without treatment, they would die very soon.

We left the mother and her children at the feeding station. Since we had the Land Rovers, I asked if we could take my aunt and other relatives back to their village. The drive took over an hour, through desolate country, so you can imagine what an effort they had made walking to see me. It was nearly dark when we arrived at their little village, but the USCRI officials wanted us to return to El Tonj for safety reasons. I had a tearful goodbye with my aunt. It had been so great to see her.

We returned to our tents in El Tonj and tried to sleep. I lay awake thinking about the starving children, wondering what had happened. I figured the doctors were giving the kids Nutriset, a milk formula to build up their strength, but I was still afraid for them. The next morning we drove to the feeding station to check on them. They were listless, but vastly improved. The baby's eyes were back, focusing on the world. It gave me the chills to see her alive once again. The mother seemed about the same. The doctors said they she had been starving for so long that she could only take in the tiniest bits of food. She told us stories about walking for weeks, carrying her children, with nothing to eat. How her friends had been raped. How she'd lost three other of her children to hunger while trying to reach the feeding station. How militias had stolen or destroyed everything she'd owned. They'd killed her husband, running him straight through with a sword. But she was alive.

And here were these magnificent volunteers risking their lives to help families like this. The war seemed so senseless, and the doctors were so selfless. They were spread out all over the countryside, in the tiniest villages. Some of them lived in the underground shelters to protect themselves from the government's bombs.

Other relief agencies had also set up centres in El Tonj. The Red Cross had a centre that served hundreds of disabled adults two meals a day, of corn porridge and beans. Another served people who, though starving, were otherwise able-bodied. They would arrive and wait patiently in queues for bowls of food. Many had no clothes, others wore only a shirt. I saw a teenager lying still on the ground, his bones poking up through his skin as a doctor slowly fed him a cup of Nutriset. In a weak voice he told the doctor that he'd walked for two weeks to reach a children's feeding centre, but because he was a teenager they'd turned him away. He walked for another three days to reach El Tonj. His parents, brothers and sisters were all dead. Before my very eyes he got stronger, from drinking the liquid, but there wasn't much more the doctor could do. When he was able to walk the doctor told him to join the other refugees, who were crowded into one of the nearby buildings. He couldn't even offer him a blanket, just another meal in the morning.

I was glad to leave the Sudan. It was too much for me to deal with. I felt tremendous guilt because I had escaped and done so well, yet millions of my countrymen were suffering. I couldn't fathom what the government was hoping to accomplish by waging this war against its own people, but I understood why the rebels didn't give up their fight. How could they give in to domination from the north?

Back in New York, my trip received a great deal of publicity. People kept telling me that before my trip was publicised, they'd had no idea what was going on in Africa. It felt incredibly good to be able to help in some small way. I had a voice, and I was using it. It made being a model worthwhile.

Over the years I've remained active with USCRI, and also with other organisations such as the United Nations High Commission for Refugees. I appeared in advertisements for their first 'Respect' campaign, with Madeleine Albright, who was secretary of state under President Clinton. That campaign used Aretha Franklin's song 'Respect' to highlight the needs of refugees. I met with First Lady Laura Bush for the Red Dress campaign, which uses images of a red dress as a symbol for the hidden prevalence of heart disease in women. The campaign encourages women to take action to wipe out the disease and protect their hearts. I've spoken in countless schools about refugees, and the need to study hard.

But nothing ever affected me as strongly as that mother and her children, literally dying for the world's attention.

CHAPTER 11

When I was twelve years old my father spoke to me from his deathbed in Khartoum.

'Alek, you must go to London. Live at peace for once. Get an education. Do well,' he said.

His words fuelled me. And now I was a successful model. I owned my own house. I had my handbag business.

In 1998 Mora left IMG, and I started working with a new agent, Maja Edmonston. I have been so lucky with my agents: Maja turned out to be a great protector of my career, just as Mora had been. I continued working all over the world and everything was going well. The only thing that suffered was my painting. After moving to New York I'd kept it for a while, but then when I started travelling so much it became difficult. I missed it terribly, because painting is very good for my soul. It soothes me and gives me a homely feeling, which is something I love. In that funny way life has of presenting you with opportunities before you even know it is happening, travelling turned out to help me with my art. I always travelled with duffel bags, which were great in that they held a lot of stuff, but they were also very awkward, as they had no pockets. I found myself thinking about bags while I was flying. About what kinds would be best for me. Then I started sketching them.

My father had carried a simple brass-clasp briefcase each day when he left the house for work. It was practical yet beautiful. That bag inspired me when I started drawing bags to pass the time on long-haul flights. It turned out that bag design was perfect for me, as it involved colour, texture and shapes, and I could do it on the run in a sketchbook, rather than having to lug around all my oils and canvases.

One week, when I wasn't travelling, I decided to make a bag at home. I ran up a bag on my old sewing machine, using some dark green cloth. I made a strap out of a black leather belt, with a buckle so you could adjust the length. It was a very simple version of a messenger bag.

I showed it to some friends, and they loved it, but it didn't even cross my mind to sell it, or produce more of them. Then, one evening, I was having dinner with a friend who was a shoe designer for Donna Karan. I told him about my bag, and he was really surprised that I'd actually made one. He asked me if I'd ever thought of designing more.

'Well yes, I'm always drawing them,' I said.

Later, I showed him my designs. He suggested I make some samples, and introduced me to a factory that would produce them.

'Just be careful,' he warned me. 'You have to know exactly what you want, and the exact sizes of the bags, or else you might waste a lot of money on mistakes.'

I was twenty-four years old and going into business, almost by accident. I realised that it was what I wanted to do. Of course, when you're a model you always wonder what will happen to you when you get too old. From that perspective, I knew the handbag company would be a good idea. I decided to finance it entirely on my own and I named it WEK1933, after my dear father and the year of his birth.

I contracted the factory to produce eighteen sample bags. I drew the patterns for the linings and took all the leather tones – chocolate brown, neutrals, dark red, dark blue, caramel – from my paintings. The hardware – the clasps and chains – was inspired by the brass jewellery one of my grand-mothers wore. I searched catalogues and the Internet and sometimes picked up unusual items.

I probably spent too much on the samples, but every bit of the business has been a learning experience, right from the beginning. At first I was the sales agent. I bought a big sample case and dragged it around from store to office to showroom, selling my wares. Amazingly, Barney's bought bags for their New York, West Coast and Japanese stores. Lagerfeld Galerie bought some. Collette, another well-known Paris boutique, bought some too. It was great. American *Vogue* and other magazines ran photos of them.

As I travelled, I'd keep notebooks of colours and textures I liked, and make notes about what feelings I had when I saw them. When I got home I'd put a piece of paper on the wall and start gathering my different ideas – sketches, and taping up pictures torn out of magazines. In time I learned to do the measurements for the bags myself so that so much wouldn't be left to the factories.

I've always run the business from my house in Brooklyn. I

have a couple of employees, young ambitious women who are great to work with. We keep it all rolling. The business isn't huge, but it's good. Everything is well-made and well-designed. I'm not looking to cash in: I want to do good-quality work and have a business that lasts a long, long time. I tell you, it feels good to see someone walking down the street carrying a WEK1933 bag.

By the time I was twenty-eight the business was sustaining itself and growing steadily. I'd done a lot of work on my house and it was very comfortable. I had a nice boyfriend, who lived in Italy but came to see me often. All in all, life was very good. But there was still one dream that nagged at me: I wanted to visit my father's grave and pay my respects to the man who was always in my heart, guiding me.

In 2004 a measure of peace had been reached in the Sudan. Various parties, including the American secretary of state Colin Powell, had gathered in Kenya to hammer out an accord between the government and the SPLA. The American participation was significant, because the Sudan had been a base for Osama bin Laden and the government also supported Saddam Hussein in the first Gulf War.

The Sudan Peace Agreement was signed in Nairobi on 9 January 2005. The accord was meant to ensure that the south would be autonomous for six years. After that, there would be a vote about whether or not the south would secede from the Sudan and form its own country. If not, then both armies – the SPLA and the government – would merge. The income from the immense oilfields in the south was to be shared equally between both regions. Northern people would get 70 per cent of national government jobs; southerners would get the remaining 30 per cent. The north would remain covered by shariah, but the Sudanese General Assembly, which included representatives from the south, would vote on whether to impose shariah on the south. It wasn't a magnificent treaty but, considering all that had preceded the signing, the thought of peace – even for just a few years – was a great relief.

For me at least.

Even as peace was arriving in Wau and the villages the government was ratcheting up the violence in Darfur, a western region of the Sudan. The area comprises three states, and is two-thirds the size of France. More than seven million people lived in Darfur, but it's believed that over a million have fled in the last few years.

Darfur is populated mostly with Muslims, although there are communities of Dinka and other animists and Christians. Many of the Muslims are dark-skinned Africans rather than Arabs. The Darfuri Arabs, partially inspired by Libya's president Muammar al-Gaddafi's notion of Arab supremacy in Africa, started to try to dominate the non-Arabs, both Muslim and non-Muslim alike. A famine in this arid, mostly roadless region led to a lot more fighting in the 1980s. Over the next fifteen years, as various rebel forces slowly developed, the government begin working with the so-called Janjaweed Arab forces. These Janjaweed forces were built from communities of Arab camel herders.

In 2003, the rebels gathered together in a convoy of thirty-three Toyota Land Cruisers and attacked a government military base at al-Fashir. They destroyed a number of planes and helicopter gunships on the ground, as well as capturing the general in charge. The rebels lost nine fighters, but killed seventy-five soldiers and technicians. This was the most serious loss in a single operation that the government had faced in the previous twenty years of war with the south.

Humiliated by this and other losses, including one where five hundred soldiers were killed, the government supplied the Janjaweed with advanced weapons and support. By the spring of the next year the Janjaweed had killed thousands of non-Arab Darfurians and driven hundreds of thousands from their villages.

A typical day went like this: the government would identify a village to be attacked. They would send in cargo planes that dropped oil barrels full of explosives. Since these 'bombs' were so crude they had no military value, other than to terrorise civilians. The bombs would be followed by helicopter gunships that strafed the buildings and fleeing civilians. Then the Janjaweed would appear on camel-back, wielding guns and swords, to finish the job by raping the women and girls, and killing the men. Arab villages were, for the most part, spared the destruction, while non-Arab villages were ruined, even when two villages, one Arab and one not, were only five hundred yards apart.

Every night the relief camps set up by aid organisations were filled with people who walked from their villages to escape the possibility of being killed in the middle of the night by raiders. In the morning they'd walk long distances back to their land to work their crops and tend their cattle. In time, over a hundred thousand refugees fled into Chad and other border countries. The world responded with rhetoric and not much else. Some people said America was preventing the UN taking action because it wanted to maintain good relations with Khartoum, so that the government didn't promise its considerable oil to the Chinese. Who knows? How can anyone explain horrors such as what has happened in Darfur? Perhaps four hundred thousand people have died. More than two million have been displaced. As I pondered the peace brokered between north and south, I wondered when peace would also come to Darfur.

With images of the Sudan constantly in the media, I felt a need to return to my homeland. It was like my second mother, calling me.

In 2004 a producer from the BBC asked me if I wanted to go to the Sudan with a documentary crew. The phone call seemed like providence. I told them I wanted to take my mother with me. We would visit my father's grave and also search for my mother's sister, Anok, whom she hadn't seen in over twenty years. No one knew if she was alive or dead.

I flew from New York to London to collect my mother and meet the crew. Walking out of Heathrow to my car, I felt protected. When I first arrived in London it seemed like the first place I'd ever really felt safe in my life. London enveloped me with peace. It was good to be back. The next day my mother and I went to a Sudanese community centre in North London to meet with the women she socialised with, along with some of my old friends from childhood. It was such a wonderful scene. The women, who were from a variety of different Dinka groups and other tribes from the Sudan, all with their own traditions, sat in a circle. They played the drums and sang, and made trilling noises as we jumped around. It was all in honour of my mother and me: they were blessing us, to send us safely on our way. It would be my mother's first trip home. These women made me proud to be a Dinka woman.

'The Sudan is my home. It's where I belong. My people are back there. So my prayers gave me always this hope that one day my country would be okay, that one day I would be allowed to return,' my mother told everyone.

I packed my boots and some medicines, and we flew the seven thousand miles to Khartoum. The city was a wreck. The tenuous peace had taken hold so recently that prosperity was still a dream. Drought and famine, in addition to the civil war, had clearly brought untold suffering to the city. As always, donkeys pulled wooden carts laden with goods, or were ridden by men in white robes. A family huddled in the decrepit hallway of an abandoned theatre, eyes heavy with the dust. The city felt like it had only recently risen from a dark dream.

We met my uncle in a café. He greeted us with hugs.

'Alek, why are you so skinny?' he asked, bemused.

'It's her job,' my mother said.

'I'm paid to be fit,' I told him.

He laughed and we drank Cokes again in this city where I had first tasted a Coca-Cola. For my mother, it was like she'd never left. She slipped right back into being Sudanese. For me, there was more of a separation. I had grown up, really, in London and New York. But still, you never forget.

My uncle smiled endlessly in his suit and tie. He was so happy to see us.

'I haven't seen my sister Anok for twenty years,' my mother said. 'Where can we find her?'

'I believe that if she's still alive she'll be in one of the villages near Wau.'

It was clear he hadn't been to the villages in a very long time.

We flew in a propeller plane across the White Nile and seven hundred miles southwest, to land on Wau's red-dirt airstrip. The airport looked so small, so primitive. In memory

206

it had been huge and complex, a modern miracle. I'd been in dozens of airports since then, but I'd never seen another one like this, with mutilated helicopter gunships and a massive crashed cargo plane dead on the edge of the runway. A group of men approached as we stepped off the plane. My mother gave them a hug. I had no idea who they were, so we exchanged a Sudanese air hug, barely touching but giving each other friendly little pats on the back. They turned out to be relatives whom I hadn't seen since I was a little girl.

Soldiers wearing camouflage and berets, carrying rifles, stood at the side of the runway. I couldn't help but be wary of them.

On the drive into town my mother and I were shocked by the damage. The road was pitted; the buildings alongside it smashed. The grand stadium that had always told me when we were getting close to the airport was crumbling. No one played there any more.

'This is not Wau,' I said to my mother.

'Not the way we remember it, no. But this is still our home,' she said.

We pulled into the front yard of a low building made of large square bricks. Two policemen stood out front.

'Mother, we never lived here, did we?' I asked as we walked towards the policeman.

'This is the house in which you were born,' she said.

I scanned the yard.

'Oh yes. Now I remember, there were flowers there, and a beautiful tree here.'

She nodded. The house was now a police station. The policemen let us into the dirty rooms.

'I remember Baba listening to the radio right there,' I said.

Baba was the name I had used for my father when I was very young. My mother's face was soft, sometimes smiling, on the verge of tears at other moments. The officers, sensing our mood, were quiet and polite.

'Goodness, how things change,' my mother said when we got back in the car and drove to our second house, the last place we lived in Wau. The zinc gate that had protected us so well from the militia one night was hanging off its hinges. We pushed it open with difficulty, then stepped through the door. Another family was living in the house. We didn't know them; the house was no longer ours. They'd built a grass-roofed hut in the yard. Our fruit trees were gone; the garden was dead. There were no cows. My mother still had cows in the village where we'd gone so many years before, descendants of the original herd. One day she was going to reclaim them. She'd recognise them in a second, she said. And she would need them in order to pay a dowry if one of my brothers married a Dinka girl. Of course, she wanted us all to marry within the Dinka tribe.

The new family showed us around. It was fun to see the old house, though I didn't feel attached to it any more and it didn't seem like it was ours. But for my mother, walking through the house was emotionally wrenching, and we didn't stay long.

'We've come to our broken home, destroyed by war,' she said to me.

Afterwards, she pointed at the houses of each our neighbours in sequence.

'I heard this lady is dead,' she said. 'That man is dead . . . this one is dead.' Then she turned and pointed to the last house. 'And this one, the teacher, she survived and is now in Canada.'

We walked to the pump where I used to collect water. The

dead bodies that had been rotting in the grass the last time I visited had gone but everything looked so shabby. Even though Wau had always been a simple town, it had changed a lot and looked really run-down.

Just then a tall woman wearing a violet-coloured outfit appeared and called out to my mother:

'Is that you Akuol?' Since there were no phones, no telegraph, no mail and no Internet, this woman, who we had known when we lived in Wau, had no way of knowing who was still alive. She'd assumed we were all dead. She burst into tears and my mother held her and stroked her hair.

Wau was now a town of refugees. The population had increased by fifty thousand since we left. Many people lived in camps. I saw a family living in a mud-walled house with a canvas roof. An old woman sat in the dirt, despondent. That could have been my mother, I thought. A young woman with a crutch and a withered leg hobbled past. That could have been me.

These people weren't begging for handouts. They wanted tools and the possibility of doing something, anything. They would find it, I knew. They were very determined people.

Further along we came to a tree where a young Dinka man was dispensing drops of polio vaccine to young children. He said he was responsible for an area the size of London. His expenses and salary were covered by Médecins Sans Frontières. Flies buzzed on some of the children's faces. They were dirty; some were naked. He had a seemingly endless, thankless job but he had such a smile. As we spoke it became clear that we were related, through my father's side. I felt so proud.

His name was Wilson Angeng. He told me that my relatives

had dispersed to every corner of the southern Sudan. My mother wondered if we would ever find her sister.

We walked up the hill, past some boys playing in the dirt with a bicycle wheel. At the top of the hill I sat down and remembered how I used to go there with my friends. We'd play and sing songs and, if we were really lucky, we'd spot a plane. I loved thinking about the exotic places they were sure to be flying to. I remembered how I dreamed of travelling the world back then.

The next morning we set off in a truck for the village of Talakong, where my mother thought we might find her sister. The driver had to avoid certain roads because he feared they still hid landmines, which were left over from the civil war. The roads we could take were rutted and difficult: it took us eight hours of steady driving to cover less than two hundred miles.

Suddenly we saw a cluster of small mud houses with conical grass roofs that looked like ice cream cones in the distance.

'That's it!' my mother said.

We were surprise visitors. My mother's father had seven wives, so her family here is quite complicated. One of her stepbrothers spotted her and came over and gave her a hug. Soon we were surrounded by relatives I'd never met. My mother tried to introduce me to everyone, but even she couldn't get them all straight. It didn't matter: they were our family and they welcomed us.

They spoke so quickly; I tried to answer as best I could, but I was so embarrassed by my Dinka, which was rusty. I knew they were thinking, What *is* this girl trying to say? My mother fitted right in. One of the young men ran off to find my mother's stepmother. When her own mother had died this woman cared for her. It is Dinka custom for the eldest member of a family to bless visitors who have been gone from the community for a long time. As we stood in the yard the chickens rustled underfoot and cattle lowed. The village seemed as alive as any city.

An old woman made her way slowly across the field. My mother became excited: there were tears in her eyes as she went up to the bent, bald woman. The woman seemed confused.

'It's Akuol,' a man said. 'Akuol, Akuol.'

'Akuol?' the old woman said, her face brightening. They hugged. Then I hugged her. She cleansed us by pouring water on our hands and our feet and by wiping our faces.

The next morning we drove to my mother's family's burial ground, where the male elders had already gathered, spears at their sides. A large steer was tethered to a stake.

'We have gathered to honour the return of our tribal daughters,' they said.

They sang and danced and jumped into the air and trilled their tongues. I feared for the cow. And, sure enough, a man recited incantations as another man took a spear and cut the cow's vein. I was horrified, once again, by this sacrifice. It is a part of my culture that I can't get used to, but I still respect it.

'It makes me feel good to have the love of my people on display,' my mother said. 'Without that we are nothing.'

Nearby were the tombs of my ancestors, set among a grove of trees. Each person had been entombed in a tall mud cone. Their names were inscribed on the side. The graves had monuments of mud made to look like almost human faces, or horns like cattle. I saw my grandfather's grave. It was an eerie sight.

'They are our fathers,' my mother said. 'The dead spirits. Whenever we call them they help us. Without them I don't think that anyone can be alive.'

I asked my ancestors to guide my mother to her sister, Anok.

I remembered Aunt Anok well. When I was four the Dinka women wanted to pierce my ears. I refused: I didn't want them to hurt me. My mother said, 'Come on, Alek. Let's get it over with.' I ran away but Aunt Anok chased me. She caught me. She pierced my ears right there.

We drove for another couple of hours, to a village where we'd heard she might be. This village had been at the epicentre of the civil war. We were afraid that everyone would be dead. We stood for a few moments in the barren village. Then my mother saw a woman walking towards us. My mother ran towards her. She threw her arms around her and burst into tears saying, 'Anok, Anok, Anok,' over and over again.

My aunt was so skinny. She looked so much older. She was missing some teeth, and others stuck out. She honestly couldn't believe her eyes. 'Akuol. Is that really you?' she said.

My aunt was so happy. She'd given up on ever seeing her sister again.

The villagers took dust and ashes from the ancestral lands and rubbed it on my face and neck to bring us together as a family with the spirits of the ancestors. They chanted and clapped their hands. They covered my mother's face with dust, blew whistles, trilled their tongues.

That night, by the fire, my mother sat on the ground and looked at me.

'So many nights we sat like this, Alek. So many nights when we were going to the village. I'd lay the blankets down and you'd sleep there with your sisters, and your brothers over there.' She pointed to different places around the fire. 'Your father there, and I was here.'

She looked into the dark forest, a faraway look in her eyes.

'In the morning, if there was no food, I'd heat up the water and tell you it was tea.'

The next day we headed back towards Wau to catch a flight to Khartoum. On the long ride across the bush my mother talked about our family and about her life.

'Your father was such a calm, strong man,' she said. 'He wanted you to know your rights. To have good values. Together he and I tried our best to make sure all nine of you got a chance in life.'

In Khartoum we rested for the night and then, in the morning, set off into the brutal heat to find my father's grave. When we arrived at the cemetery my mother looked confused. Everything was different.

'What's happened here?' she asked the caretaker.

'A lot of dead people,' he said. 'There have been too many dead people in these last years.'

The graveyard was now a vast dry field of graves, without a bush, blade of grass or flower in sight. Some of the dead were buried in cement boxes that rose high above the ground. Others were in wooden boxes in the dirt with their names written in paint on sticks in the ground. My father had been buried in the ground, in a cement crypt. I'd never seen it, because children weren't allowed to visit the dead.

My mother looked distraught as we walked among the

graves, afraid she wouldn't find my father. We wandered for an hour. She became desperate. Then, suddenly, something looked familiar in the old section of the graveyard. There was my father's grave, his name etched into the cement.

I felt so low. My mother burst into tears.

I held her and then we both straightened up. She spoke:

'I have come with your child to see your grave. War sent us far away to seek safety for ourselves. Now the children are all well. Alek is here now. She has done very well. I want your spirit to stay with our children and bless them. We searched a long time for your grave. We thought we'd never find it, but now we're here. I beg you to look after our children—'

I began to sob.

'So they can lead good lives.'

Life had shown me that he would.